WORLD WAR II FLASHBACK

WORLD WAR II FLASHBACK
A Fact-Filled Look at the War Years

Timothy B. Benford

Longmeadow Press

Other Books by Timothy B. Benford

Nonfiction
Righteous Carnage (True Crime)
The World War II Quiz & Fact Book, Vol. 1
The World War II Quiz & Fact Book, Vol. 2
The Space Program Quiz & Fact Book
The Royal Family Quiz & Fact Book

Fiction
Hitler's Daughter
The Ardennes Tapes

COVER PHOTO:
The USS Arizona *(BB-39) burns helplessly during the Japanese attack on Pearl Harbor, December 7, 1941. Photo courtesy of the Arizona Memorial Museum Association, 1 Arizona Memorial Place, Honolulu, Hawaii 96818.*

Published by Longmeadow Press, 201 High Ridge Road, Stamford, CT 06904.

Cover and Interior design by Allan Mogel

Layout by Timothy B. Benford

ISBN: 0-681-41181-3

Printed in the United States of America

0 9 8 7 6 5 4 3 2 1

Dedicated to the memory of the late

Michael W. Benford

wounded in action aboard the

USS Emmons (DD-457),

sunk at Okinawa, April 6, 1945

and

Sam Austin Benford

who along with

1,176 others perished aboard the

USS Arizona (BB-39)

December 7, 1941

Acknowledgments

A book of this scope would have been impossible to attempt without the generous contributions and assistance of literally hundreds of veterans and civilians who lived through the war years. For them these pages contain more than a flashback—they contain personal experiences and memories.

I extend my sincere appreciation to the following individuals for their contributions: George M. Barclay; Mrs. Kenneth L. Boughner; William H. Buchanan; Joe De Caro; Charles E. (Bud) Hilton, Jr.; John A Hutchinson; Ben Lebowitz; Murray D. Lombardo; Ms. Renee Brown Lovato; Joseph Niechwiadowicz; Larry Platt; George Schroth; Robert J. Schwartz; James W. Vernon, Ph.D; Mrs. Frank F. Wall; David Westheimer; and Harold D. Zahler.

I would particularly like to thank Mrs. Robert Goralski, who gave me access to the voluminous photo file her late husband compiled while working on his *World War II Almanac*. Bob's photos, along with my own and those from the people just mentioned, provided me with in excess of 1,000 photographs to choose from.

Several of the photographs in this book have not been previously published. They are the contributions from combat photographers, veterans or their families. I am proud to present them here for the first time.

Two final mentions of thanks: to Heide Lange, my literary agent at Sanford J. Greenburger Associates, and Daniel Bial, my editor first at Harper & Row and now at Longmeadow Press. Their confidence, professional guidance and assistance made this an enormously pleasant project.

CONTENTS

THE WAR ON LAND

The first U.S. Army division to secure a beachhead during the Normandy invasion on D-Day was the 4th Infantry Division, on Utah Beach. Today remnants of German gun emplacements and various vehicles behind Utah and other beaches are popular with tourists.
—Photo by author

1

The first Allied troops, other than airborne, to invade Europe on D-Day were 132 men from the U.S. 4th and 24th Cavalry squadrons. They invaded a pair of islands, Îles-St. Marcouf, about three miles off Utah Beach at 4:30 A.M. During the complicated planning for Operation Overlord the islands had failed to attract any attention. However, as D-Day neared, the Allied command determined that these islands could be the sites of heavy German gun batteries. The American invaders found no enemy troops or gun emplacements. Nonetheless, the troops sustained casualties (19 killed or wounded) from a labyrinth of mine fields. Perhaps the most widely seen photo of D-Day is the accompanying picture of U.S. troops going ashore shortly after the invasion began. It was taken by an unnamed U.S. Coast Guard photographer and captioned "Into the Jaws of Death."

—U.S. Coast Guard photo

The First United States Army Group (FUSAG) was the fictitious military formation that the Allies wanted the Germans to think was under the command of General George S. Patton and would spearhead the invasion of Europe. Patton was the Allied general the Germans respected above all others, and they simply couldn't believe the Allies would not use him to lead the D-Day invasion. Consequently, the German high command waited for "Army Group Patton" (or FUSAG) to storm the beaches at Pas de Calais instead of what they considered the diversionary action at Normandy. Neither Patton nor the imaginary FUSAG took part in the invasion.

★★★★★

Before the war was over, General George S. Patton was able to boast that his army had liberated more square miles of Europe, traveled farther, and caused more German casualties than any other Allied army.

★★★★★

The only area of the Benedictine monastery of Monte Casino in Italy to survive the devastating Allied bombing was the crypt where St. Benedict is buried. General von Senger und Etterlin, the German commander responsible for defending Monte Casino, was a lay member of the Benedictine order.

★★★★★

The first Allied invasion and airborne forces to link up on D-Day were from the 101st Airborne and the U.S. 4th Infantry, behind Utah Beach. The 101st had its first exchange of gunfire with the Germans at the French village of Foucarville, when 11 troopers attacked machine gun, anti–tank gun and dugout positions.

★★★★★

The first British civilian casualties were in the Orkney Islands on March 16, 1940.

The heaviest concentration of German troops on D-Day was at La Roche–Guyon, the headquarters of Field Marshall Erwin Rommel's Army Group B, the most powerful military presence in France. There were more than three soldiers for every villager.

★★★★★

The only German troops in France that did not receive the alert from German intelligence to expect the Allied invasion of France "within 48 hours" was the Seventh Army, commanded by Colonel General Friedrich Dollman. His sector of responsibility included the five Normandy beaches the Allies called Omaha, Utah, Gold, Juneau, and Sword.

★★★★★

The first SS general to be given command of an army was General Paul Hausser, who commanded the 7th Army during the Normandy invasion. He had been a lieutenant general in the regular army before joining the SS.

★★★★★

The first and last German generals promoted to field marshall by Hitler were Werner von Blomberg in 1936 and Ritter von Greim in 1945. In all Hitler promoted 25 of his 3,363 generals to field marshall rank. The U.S. had just over 1,500 generals during the war.

★★★★★

The highest-ranking traitor in the war was Soviet General Andrei Andreyevitch Vlasov, a hero during the German attack on Moscow. Captured by the Germans, he cast his lot with them and built up an army of Soviet prisoners who fought for Germany until May 1945. Captured for a second time, this time by General George S. Patton's troops, Vlasov was turned over to the Soviets, who promptly hanged him.

U.S. 82nd Airborne Division General James M. Gavin was the first American general on French soil on D-Day, having "dropped in" four-and-a-half hours before the invasion from the sea began. The only Allied general to land with the first wave in the amphibious invasion at Normandy on D-Day was U.S. Brigadier General Theodore Roosevelt, son of the former President, who landed with the 4th Division. (*NOTE:* General Roosevelt and his son, Captain Quentin Roosevelt, were the only father and son team to participate in the invasion on June 6. Quentin came ashore at Omaha Beach.)
—*U.S. Army photo*

The first ever combat for U.S. paratroopers was in August 1942, but it didn't involve the famed 82nd Airborne, the All American Division, or the Screaming Eagles of the 101st Airborne. The U.S. Marine Corps 1st Parachute Battalion gained the distinction when they landed on the northeast coast of Gavutu Island. Purists will quickly point out that this action, however, was an amphibious invasion rather than an airborne drop.

★★★★★

The first combat jump of the 101st Airborne Division was not until the Normandy invasion on June 6, 1944. Along with the 82nd Airborne, 882 planes brought 13,000 men from both divisions to six drop zones within a few miles of Ste.-Mère-Église, France.

★★★★★

The first British general to land during D-Day was Major General Richard (Windy) Gale, commander of the 6th Airborne, with reinforcements for troopers who had landed at the Caen Canal and Orne River bridges. A year earlier British paratrooper strength had been deemed sufficient to organize and equip two airborne divisions, the 1st and this one. The designation as number "6" for Gale's troopers was chosen to confuse the Germans.

★★★★★

The first U.S. airborne officer killed in combat was Lieutenant Walter W. Kiser, USMC, on August 7, 1942, when the 1st Parachute Battalion landed on the northeast coast of Gavutu in the Solomon Islands. Gavutu, along with Tulagi and Florida Islands, were satellites around Guadalcanal, the much bigger objective. The overriding reason for the invasion of Guadalcanal was to prevent Japan from completing an air base there that would threaten Australia with land-based bombers.

The first U.S. Army paratrooper killed in combat was Private John T. MacKall, who was enroute to the North Africa theater of operations when a French fighter attacked the aircraft he was in.

★★★★★

The first major training ground of U.S. airborne "pathfinder" units was at Biscari Airfield in Sicily. The invasion of Sicily had been spearheaded by the 82nd Airborne Division's 505th Parachute Regimental Combat Team on July 9, 1943.

★★★★★

The first airborne attack using sappers was the German assault on Fort Eben Emael, Belgium, in May 1940. It was commanded by Captain Walter Koch. His engineer troops captured nine installations during the first 10 minutes in what was considered the strongest fort in the world. Koch and his 424 men used 42 gliders in the offensive.

★★★★★

The Molotov cocktail was *not* created by the Russians to honor Soviet Foreign Minister V. I. Molotov, nor did it make its debut in World War II. The first reported use of ignited bottles containing gasoline being hurled at enemy tanks was in the Spanish Civil War (1936–39). The lethal concoction got its name, however, from Finnish troops during the 1939–40 Winter War against the Soviets. In actuality, the Molotov cocktail was something of a weapon of last resort and only used when Finnish troops found themselves hard pressed to halt or slow down the tide of Soviet tanks against them. By the time the four-month campaign ended, the Finns had destroyed more than 2,300 Soviet tanks. At the outbreak of hostilities with its giant neighbor to the east the Finnish liquor industry provided the army with approximately 100,000 fifth-size bottles.

The first German to sight and report the Allied armada as it approached the Normandy beaches on D-Day was Major Werner Pluskat, who commanded four batteries of the German 352nd Division with its 20 guns facing the water. When asked where the Allied ships were heading, he replied, "Right for me!" His vantage point was a bunker above Omaha Beach.

—Photos by author

General Dwight D. Eisenhower's first choice to command the 21st Army Group for Operation Overlord, the Normandy invasion, was not General Bernard Law Montgomery. Ike considered him an inadequate strategist and preferred instead British General Sir Harold Alexander. However, Prime Minister Winston S. Churchill had other plans for Alexander and overruled Ike. Churchill hoped that Alexander, as commander of the 15th Army Group in Italy, could take Rome and eventually open the way to the Balkans. As a result the 21st Army Group was given to Montgomery.
—U.S. Army photo

The first French town captured by the Allies after the Normandy invasion in June 1944 was Carentan. In contrast, the Allies bypassed and specifically avoided selected areas of France as they pushed toward Germany. The two French ports of Lorient and St.-Nazaire remained under German occupation until they surrendered at the end of the war. This photo shows U.S. troops moving through Carentan streets and away from St.-Lô and Paris.

—U.S. Army photo

The first German city captured by American troops was Aachen, on October 21, 1944, after bitter fighting. The city is famous in history as the fortress of Charlemagne.

★★★★★

The last person to be incarcerated in the Tower of London was Deputy Reichführer Rudolf Hess, who was captured when he flew to Scotland on May 10, 1941. At the time Hess was second in power only to Hitler in Nazi Germany. Hess told his captors his mission was a peace overture to Britain. After the war he was convicted and sentenced to life in prison during the Nuremberg war crimes trials, and he became the last war prisoner held captive in Spandau Prison outside Berlin. He died there in 1987.

★★★★★

The first Japanese withdrawal after an unsuccessful amphibious landing was at Milne Bay, New Guinea, in August 1942.

★★★★★

The first land operation in Europe was an unsuccessful mission by British commandos on June 24–25, 1940, around Boulogne, France. The objective was to observe German defenses and capture and return with military personnel for questioning in this regard. However, the British were unable to capture alive either of the two Germans they encountered and returned with information that was considered of marginal importance.

★★★★★

The last U.S. Marine to leave Wake Island in 1941 was Colonel Walter Bayler, who made his exit aboard a U.S. Navy PBY on December 21, 1941. He was also the first Marine to set foot back on Wake after the Japanese surrender in September 1945.

The first British combat personnel to join the Greeks fighting the Italians landed in Greece on November 3, 1940. The vanguard consisted of Royal Air Force and British army troops. Three days later RAF bombers conducted their first raid, against the Italian air base in Valona, Albania.

★★★★★

The last mounted cavalry action by the U.S. was the January 1942 charge by the 26th Cavalry Regiment against the Japanese in the Philippines. It occurred as U.S. forces were retreating to Bataan. During the siege of the fortress cavalry horses were slaughtered for food. (The cavalry remained a functioning part of the U.S. armed forces throughout the war with the continued operation of the cavalry school at Fort Reilly, Kans.

★★★★★

Only four of Germany's 90 infantry divisions were totally motorized at the outbreak of war. Horsepower, literally, moved the other 86. On September 1, 1939, Germany depended on more than a half-million horses to support its troops. According to Wehrmacht records, a well-equipped German division included 4,842 horses versus 1,009 automobiles and trucks, whereas a sparsely equipped division contained more than 6,000 horses but fewer than 600 automobiles and trucks. By the end of the war slightly more than 2.7 million horses had been used by Germany on all fronts.

★★★★★

The 1st Marine Division made the first beachhead on Peleliu Island on September 15, 1944. It was a campaign in which progress was gauged in yards, sometimes feet. The U.S. Army sent troops from the 81st Division to assist the Marines on September 23, but

The first British engagement in France on D-Day was the glider-commando attack by 181 troops against Benouville Bridge over the Caen Canal (renamed Pegasus Bridge afterward) and bridges over the adjacent Orne River. This air reconnaissance photo taken at 6 A.M. on D-Day shows that three British gliders had landed within yards of Pegasus Bridge.

—British 6th Airborne photo

Pegasus Bridge →

Pegasus Bridge as it appears today.
—*Photo by author*

In the top photo Australian troops in Bren carriers are seen moving en mass across the North African desert while in the bottom photo an unlucky Italian tank crew comes to the realization that it will be sitting out the rest of the war in Allied hands.
—Imperial War Museum photos

The first contact between British and German troops in North Africa was in Libya on February 27, 1941. Rommel's first offensive against the British was the March 24, 1941, attack by the 5th Light Division against El Agheila in Libya, which fell with little resistance.

★★★★★

The first British offensive in North Africa was against the Italians and Libyans at Sidi Barrâni on December 9, 1940, and resulted in the recapture of the city two days later. Lieutenant General Sir Richard O'Connor's 31,000 troops of the Western Desert Force engaged and captured more than 38,000 of the 80,000 troops under Marshall Rodolfo Graziani, including three divisions.

★★★★★

The first major Axis offensive in North Africa occurred on September 13, 1940, when a superior force of five Italian and Libyan divisions from bases in Libya attacked lightly fortified British advance positions at Sollum, Egypt. The British wisely withdrew in the face of overwhelming opposition as the invaders continued the penetration some 50 miles to Sidi Barrâni, Egypt.

★★★★★

The campaign that is considered the most spectacular series of victories ever gained over a British army was the successful German capture of Tobruk in 1942.

★★★★★

The British Second Army, under Sir Miles Dempsey, had the greatest representation of foreign units in it. Besides British army troops it included American, Irish, Scottish, Polish, Czech, Belgian, and Dutch troops.

The last German panzer offensive in North Africa was at Djebel Bou-Aoukaz on April 30, 1943.

★★★★★

The first British victory over the Germans was the offensive against El Agheila, Libya, on January 6, 1942. The British Eighth Army caused nearly 40,000 German casualties.

★★★★★

The highest-paid armed forces in the war were the Americans. A U.S. Army staff sergeant earned as much as a British army captain. A U.S. private serving overseas earned $60 per month, roughly three times as much as his British counterpart. This sometimes led to friction. The British quip "You Yanks are overpaid, oversexed, and over here" earned the American response "You Brits are underpaid, undersexed, and under Eisenhower!"

★★★★★

The first U.S. land victory against the Japanese was at Guadalcanal. The invasion, which began on August 7, 1942, was also the first major amphibious assault in the Pacific.

★★★★★

The first battle in which the Japanese defended territory they had held prior to the war was in the campaign for the island of Kwajalein in January 1944.

★★★★★

The only British ground commander to hold the distinction of never having lost a battle was General, later Field Marshall, Bernard Law Montgomery.

The first U.S. tank ashore during the amphibious landing of the U.S. 5th Marine Division at Kyushu, Japan, was tank number 30 of A Company. It is seen here at Sasebo Naval Base with infantry members from the 26th Regiment hitching a ride.

—U.S. Army photo

The first units of Patton's Third Army to cross the Rhine were aboard the tank Flat Foot Floosie of the 41st Tank Battalion, 11th Armored Division. They reached Oppenheim, near Mainz, on Thursday, March 22, 1945. The crew was, left to right: Corporal William Hasse, Palisades Park, N.J.; Private Marvin Aldridge, Burlington, N.C.; T/4 John Latimi, Bronx, N.Y.; Corporal Vincent Morreale, Trenton, N.J.; and Corporal Sidney Meyer, Bronx, N.Y.

—U.S. Army photo

The first three Allied tanks to enter Paris during the City of Light's liberation in August 1944 were named after Napoleon's battles: Montmirail, Romilly, and Champaubert. The tanks, which clanked along the same route Bonaparte had taken in his return from Elba, were under the command of Captain Raymond Dronne. In the photo the first tank passes through the Porte d'Italie (the Italian Door) entrance to the city.

—*U.S. Army photo*

The greatest tank battle in history took place between the Germans and Soviets, July 4–12, 1943, at the Kursk salient in the Soviet Union. More than 6,300 tanks and assault guns from both sides were involved. The Germans moved 900,000 men in 16 panzer and motorized divisions that included 2,700 tanks and assault guns, plus 34 other divisions along a front that was 345 miles wide. They faced Soviet opposition that included 155 pieces of artillery *per mile,* 3,600 tanks and assault guns, and 1.3 million men. In the first two days the German Fourth Panzer alone lost just over 200 tanks while advancing only six miles. However, the "Mother of All Tank Battles" took place on July 12 when more than 1,500 German and Soviet tanks faced each other in a shootout reminiscent of the Old West, blasting away at each other from point-blank range. Each side suffered 50 percent casualties. Additional fighting continued for more than a month as the Soviets pressed the campaign against the retreating Germans.

★★★★★

The largest tanks built in the war were a pair of 185-ton, 30-foot-long German giants appropriately called Mammoths. (By comparison, the heaviest Allied tank was the 43.1-ton British Mark IV Churchill.) Designed by automaker Ferdinand Porsche, they had steel plating 9.5 inches thick. Tested in June 1944, they ruined any roads they were driven on, crushing cobblestone into powder. When they traveled on dirt roads, they sank deep into the earth. Never used in combat, they were destroyed at Kümmersdorf in late 1944 so that they wouldn't fall into the hands of the advancing Allies.

★★★★★

The U.S. produced the greatest number of tanks of any nation in the war: 61,000 among five models. Italy produced the fewest tanks, 2,100 (see complete tank chart in appendix).

The only French division in France when the 1st Army liberated Paris in August 1944 was the 2nd French Armored, which headed the advance on the city.

★★★★★

The tank style produced in greater numbers than any other was the 37.1-ton, 19.3-foot-long M3A1 Sherman. The U.S. produced more than 49,000. The lowest production for tanks that saw combat was the 74.8-ton, 22.3-foot-long German Elephant. Fewer than 100 were made.

★★★★★

The first member of the U.S. military to set foot in Tokyo after hostilities ceased was Admiral Lewis Smith-Parks, commander of Submarine Squadron Twenty. Smith-Parks, who participated in the surrender ceremonies in Tokyo Bay, made a secret visit to the emperor's palace before General Douglas MacArthur's formal visit.

★★★★★

The first public announcement of the formation of the Free French government in exile was made by General Charles de Gaulle on radio, from London, on October 27, 1940.

★★★★★

The most powerful of the various Resistance groups in France, both in terms of military might and political clout, was the communist FTP (Francs-Tireurs et Partisans).

★★★★★

The last European capital in Hitler's "Fortress Europe" to be liberated by the Allies was Prague, Czechoslovakia, in May 1945.

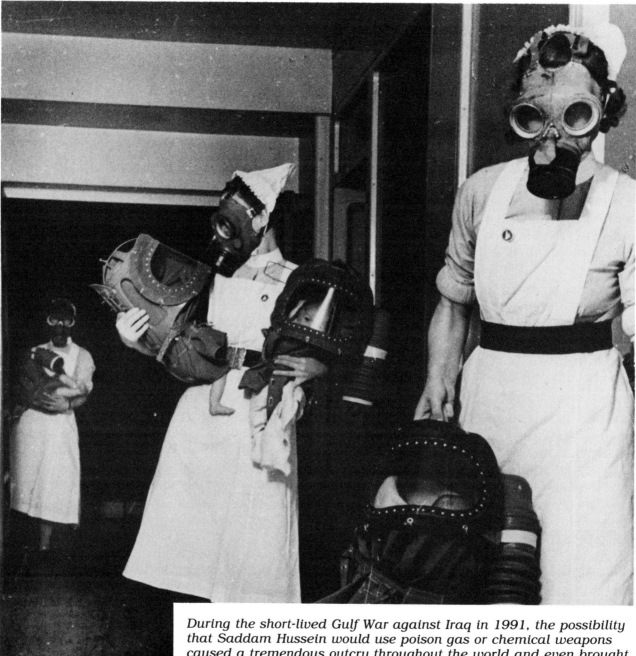

During the short-lived Gulf War against Iraq in 1991, the possibility that Saddam Hussein would use poison gas or chemical weapons caused a tremendous outcry throughout the world and even brought preemptive condemnation of such actions from nations considered sympathetic to Iraq. On September 30, 1939, the British war cabinet authorized shipping poison gas to France for use against German troops in the event Germany used chemicals first. Eleven days later Britain quadrupled its production of mustard gas to 1,200 tons per

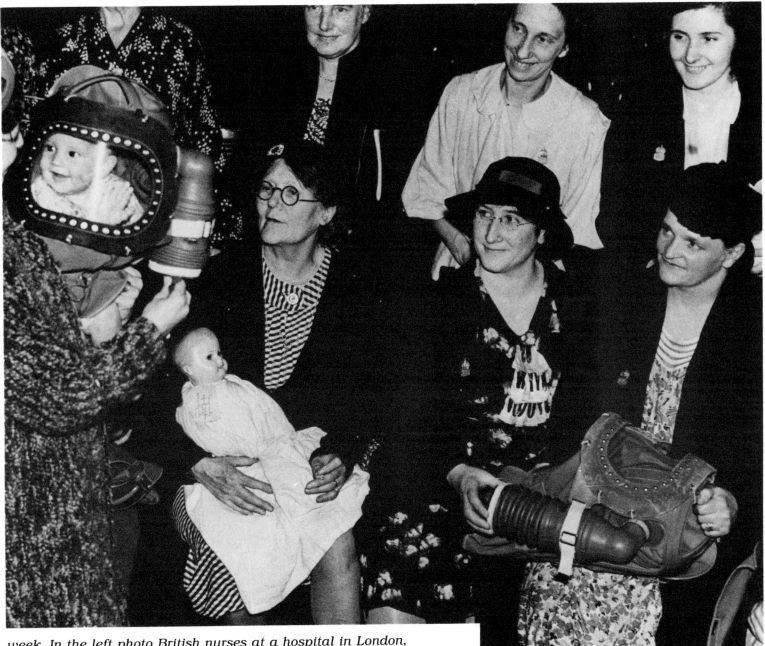

week. In the left photo British nurses at a hospital in London, themselves wearing gas masks, are seen with infants in spacelike chemical protection suits. In the photo above mothers and grandmothers attend a class to learn proper use of the special suits for young children.

—Imperial War Museum photo
—Courtesy of Mrs. Robert Goralski

*The highest-ranking German officer captured in North Africa was
General Jurgen von Arnim, seen here following his surrender of
238,243 German and Italian troops (all Axis forces in the theater) in
Tunis and Bizerte on May 12, 1942. The highest-ranking Italian officer
captured was Field Marshall Alessandro Messe.*

—U.S. Army photo

20

The last commander of the Afrika Korps was General Gustav Fehn. The Afrika Korps ceased to exist as a fighting unit when all Axis forces in North Africa surrendered on May 12, 1942. Contrary to popular belief, the Afrika Korps did not identify the entire German force in North Africa but only two divisions: the 15th and 21st Panzer (formerly 5th Light). Erwin Rommel was never listed as commander of the Afrika Korps. He was, in fact, commander of the larger, overall force, which included the two divisions of the Korps along with the German 90th Light Division and six Italian divisions under his direct command. According to German military records, when Rommel first arrived in North Africa in February 1941, he was listed as commander of the *Deutschen Truppen in Libyen* (German troops in Libya).

★★★★★

The first German general to become a casualty after the Allied invasion of Normandy was General Wilhelm Falley, commander of the 91st Infantry Division. He was fatally wounded by members of the U.S. 508th Parachute Infantry Regiment on D-Day, June 6, 1944.

★★★★★

The only U.S. Marine Corps officer to ever command a field army was Major General Roy S. Geiger, a naval aviator. Geiger was second in command to U.S. General Simon B. Buckner when the army officer was killed during the battle for Okinawa. Geiger immediately assumed command of the Tenth Army.

★★★★★

The only person in the war to receive a dishonorable discharge from one branch of the service and then become a general in another was Nazi Reinhard Heydrich. He had been thrown out of the German navy but was made welcome in the SS.

The first U.S. Marine Corps officer to attain four stars was General Thomas Holcomb, commander of the corps from 1936–44.

★★★★★

The youngest general in the German army was Walter Wenck, 45, commander of the 12th Army and former chief of staff to General Heinz Guderian. The youngest general in the Luftwaffe was Adolf Galland, who was promoted to the rank in 1942 when he was 30 years old.

★★★★★

At age 50, Erwin Rommel was the youngest field marshall in the war or, for that matter, in German history. Hitler elevated Rommel to the rank after his stunning successes in North Africa against the British. At the presentation Hitler gave Rommel an 18-inch-long gold baton that weighed three pounds. The field marshall was never seen publicly with it after that.

★★★★★

The highest bounty ever put on a human being is the $1 million reward offered for the capture of Adolf Hitler by U.S. industrialist Samuel H. Church in 1940. The conditions were that Hitler be alive and unharmed and that he be tried by an international court set up by the League of Nations.

★★★★★

The most decorated soldier in World War II, and in U.S. history, was Audie Murphy, who had received the Medal of Honor and 27 other decorations by the time he was 20 years old. After the war Murphy wrote about his wartime experiences in the book *To Hell and Back* and played himself in the subsequent movie. In the 1950s he appeared in a number of Westerns.

THE FIRST ACROSS THE RHINE

CONSTRUCTED BY
• 291 ENGR C BN
• 988 TDWY CO
• 998 TDWY CO

THE LONGEST TACTICAL BRIDGE BUILT

The first American soldier to cross the Rhine and set foot on German soil was Sargeant Alexander A. Drabik, a butcher from Holland, Ohio, who led a platoon from the 9th Armored Division, First Army, across the Ludendorff Bridge at Remagen and through a barrage of artillery fire at 4 P.M. on March 7, 1944. In the photo above, Private Leroy Johnson of Lakewood, N.Y., operates a traffic control telephone to direct vehicles and troops across the treadway pontoon bridge from Remagen to Erpel, Germany, on March 17, the same day the Ludendorff Bridge crumbled.

—U.S. Army photo

The Ludendorff Bridge at Remagen, Germany, the only Rhine crossing that had not been destroyed, collapsed 10 days after the first Allied troops began to cross it in March 1945. Four hours after this photo was taken on March 17, the bridge crumbled. Some 400 troops of the U.S. First Army were on it at the time.

—*U.S. Army photo*

The first German army surrender to U.S. troops occurred on May 9, 1945 (one day after the official end of the war in Europe), when General Gustav von Vaerst, commander of the Fifth Panzer Army, handed his pistol to General Omar Bradley. Prior to that, however, U.S. troops had captured German units up to battalion size and large segments of decimated divisions. The thousands of prisoners shown here were captured in the Ruhr in April 1945.

—U.S. Army photo

The greatest number of enemy troops captured in one place at one time was Germany's capture of more than 660,000 Soviet troops at Kiev on September 16, 1941. (Soviet figures claim it was only 527,000.)

★★★★★

The first German army to surrender in the war was the Sixth Army, under Friedrich von Paulus, which surrendered to the Soviets at Stalingrad on January 31, 1943. A day earlier Paulus had been promoted to field marshall by Hitler. On learning of the surrender, the Nazi leader said: "Paulus did an about-face on the threshold of immortality!"

★★★★★

The most decorated Philippine soldier in the war was future president Ferdinand E. Marcos. Stories have circulated that many of his exploits were fictitious and that he connived to be awarded his medals in order to get fame and political advantage.

★★★★★

The youngest American general in the war was 34-year-old Brigadier General Gerald J. Higgins of the 101st Airborne Division.

★★★★★

The first U.S. outpost to fall into enemy hands in the war was the island of Guam. The largest of the Marianas Islands chain, Guam was also the most populous, with 60,000 inhabitants. On December 10, 1941, a 6,000-man Japanese invasion force overwhelmed fewer than 500 armed defenders, who included U.S. Marines, sailors, and native constabulary. The defenders, who had nothing larger than a .30-caliber machine gun, suffered 17 killed versus 10 for the invaders. Guam was not recaptured until August 1944.

The U.S. sustained a greater number of casualties during one campaign, the Battle of the Bulge, than were suffered by U.S. forces under General Douglas MacArthur throughout the entire war. Nearly 12,000 out of 16,000 troops of the 106th U.S. Infantry Division were killed, wounded, or captured by the Germans in the Ardennes Forest just before Christmas 1944.

★★★★★

The most decorated unit in U.S. history was the 442nd Regimental Combat Team, whose motto was Go for Broke. It consisted of Japanese-American volunteers, who won 4,667 major medals, awards, and citations, including 560 Silver Stars, 28 of which had oak-leaf clusters; 4,000 Bronze Stars; 52 Distinguished Service Crosses; one Congressional Medal of Honor; and 54 other decorations. This unit also held the distinction of never having a case of desertion. The majority of soldiers in the 442nd served while their relatives in the U.S. were being held in the infamous detention centers and camps created as a result of the panic after Pearl Harbor.

★★★★★

The last major amphibious operation of the war was the invasion of Okinawa, in which 60,000 U.S. troops (two Marine and two Army divisions) were involved. The closest American flag to the Japanese home islands was raised on the northern end of Okinawa in mid-April 1945 by the U.S. 6th Marine Division. It was the same flag they had raised on the southern end on June 21.

★★★★★

The highest rate of casualties ever sustained by a U.S. Marine Corps regiment in one battle was 2,821 out of 3,512 Marines from the 29th Regiment in the 82 days of the Okinawa campaign in 1945.

U.S. First Army Second Lieutenant William D. Robertson of Los Angeles, acclaimed as the first American to meet the Soviets at Torgau, Germany, on April 25, 1945, re-created the rendezvous with Lieutenant Alexander Sylvachko for the camera.

—U.S. Army photo

Our greetings to the brave troops of the First Amerikan Army

The first official linkup between American and Soviet troops on the battlefield came at 4:40 P.M. on April 25 on the Elbe River in Torgau, Germany. Lieutenant William D. Robertson of Los Angeles, U.S. 69th Division, First Army, met soldiers of Marshall Koniev's First Ukranian Army on the twisted and sloping girders of a blown-out bridge spanning the Elbe. However, Lieutenant Albert Kotzebue and a patrol, also of the U.S. 69th, crossed the Elbe three hours earlier at 1:30 P.M. the same day and reported meeting Soviet soldiers in Strehla. The top photo shows Robertson and a Soviet lieutenant named Sylvashko reinacting their initial embrace. The photo below captures American and Soviet officers dancing with women of the Red Army following dinner to celebrate the historic meeting.

—U.S. Army photo

The most powerful artillery gun used by any nation during the war was a German monster named Karl (after its designer Karl Becker). Its two-and-a-half-ton shells were 24 inches wide, could travel three miles, and were capable of penetrating eight to nine feet of concrete. Karl was used on the Eastern Front against the Soviets.
—U.S. Army photo

The largest artillery piece ever built was the 80-centimeter German *Schwere Gustav* (Heavy Gustav), which was used for the first, and last, time in the bombardment of the Soviet port city of Sevastopol in June 1942. The 1,350-ton monster, which traveled on railroad tracks, had a barrel length of 29 meters and a range of 47 kilometers and fired 7,100-kilogram concrete-piercing shells. It required 2,000 men to be set up and fired. Moving Gustav from Germany to Sevastopol involved a work crew of 1,500 laborers and engineers to prepare railroad beds in advance. Gustav was only one of several big guns that Germany used against Sevastopol. The city was hit by no fewer than 562,944 artillery projectiles in what is recorded as one of the heaviest bombardments of all time. Ironically, Gustav fired only 48 rounds in the Sevastopol campaign and, perhaps because of the manpower needed and logistics involved, never saw action again.

The first hostile action against Canadian territory was in June 1942 by a Japanese submarine firing at Vancouver Island. There were no injuries.

★★★★★

The first major airborne operation independent of other armed forces support was the May 20, 1940, German assault on Crete.

★★★★★

The worst military disaster ever suffered by an Allied nation in the Pacific/Orient was the February 15, 1942, fall of Singapore. The Japanese captured more than 70,000 British troops and civilians.

★★★★★

The first Japanese beachhead in the Philippines campaign in 1941 was at Aparri, north of Luzon.

★★★★★

The final phase of the German Battle for France, which began as the Dunkirk evacuation ended, was code-named Operation Red.

★★★★★

The first British officer to receive a Victorian Cross was Army Captain Harold Ervine-Andrews of the Lancastershire Regiment, for heroic action at Dunkirk in 1940.

★★★★★

The only amphibious invasion thrown back with a loss in the war was the first Japanese attempt to take Wake Island on December 11, 1941. They were successful, however, on their second try a short time later.

The largest U.S. land campaign of the war in the Pacific was the fight for Lingayen Gulf and Luzon, the Philippines, in 1944. More U.S. troops were involved than had participated in North Africa or Italy.

★★★★★

The U.S. Marine to receive the last Medal of Honor authorized by Congress *during* the war was Pfc. Robert M. McTureous, Jr., for action on Okinawa. (Medals of Honor were authorized to other veterans after hostilities ceased.)

★★★★★

The first German soldier was killed in occupied Paris in 1942 at the Barbes Metro station. He was shot by a Frenchman, Pierre Fabien, who was captured and executed by the Germans.

★★★★★

The last Polish regular army troops to surrender after the German invasion did so at Warsaw on September 17, 1939, only 16 days after the start of the invasion.

★★★★★

The only U.S. corps commander in the war who was a National Guard officer was Major General Raymond S. McLain, who commanded the XIX Corps.

★★★★★

The highest-ranking Canadian overseas commander was General Andrew G. McNaughton.

★★★★★

The first Australian and New Zealand (ANZAC) troops arrived in Egypt on February 13, 1940.

The first segregated black American infantry troops to fight in the South Pacific theater as a unit were members of the 93rd Division, 1st Battalion, 25th Combat Team, who saw action in Bougainville in April 1944. Soldiers in the photo with their backs to camera are advancing on Hill 165 while those in the second photo are seen in the area of the Numa-Numa Trail.

—U.S. Army photos

The first non-Chinese general ever to command Chinese troops was U.S. Army General Joseph W. (Vinegar Joe) Stilwell, who commanded the Chinese Fifth and Sixth armies in Burma in 1942. Waiting to board an aircraft that will take them to Chungking, China, in this September 1944 photo are Stilwell, Major General Patrick J. Hurley, and Major General Daniel I. Sultan.

—U.S. Army photo

The first U.S. Army activated overseas during the war was the Fifth Army under General Mark Clark. When the Fifth Army captured Rome in June 1944, it was only the third time in history that the Eternal City had been successfully assaulted from the south: the first time was in A.D. 536 by Belisarius of the Eastern Empire, and the feat was not duplicated until 1849, when Giuseppe Garibaldi marched up the boot and ended papal rule.

—U.S. Army photo

The last major amphibious invasion of the war was Okinawa on Easter Sunday, April 1, 1945. U.S. Marine Corporal Fenwick H. Dunn, 19, gives the candy from his K rations to an aged woman on Okinawa.

—U.S. Marine Corps photo

Bernard Law Montgomery was not Britain's first choice to command
the Eighth Army in North Africa against Rommel. He was selected as
a replacement after Lieutenant General W. H. E. Gott, handpicked by
Prime Minister Winston Churchill, was killed in a plane crash on
August 8, 1942. By the time Monty and U.S. General William K.
Harrison, Jr., exchanged pleasantries in England in April 1944, the
field marshall had become a British living legend.
—U.S. Army photo

The first attempt on Hitler's life after the war began was on November 9, 1939. Hitler had left a Munich beer hall some 20 minutes before a bomb attached to a supporting pillar exploded, killing nine people. The Führer is seen here in 1941 relaxing with a wirehaired terrier at his East Prussia headquarters after Operation Barbarossa, the invasion of Russia, began.
—U.S. Army, photo from the Von Ribbentrop albums
—Courtesy of Mrs. Robert Goralski

The first armed resistance in the Warsaw ghetto was on January 18, 1943. The first Jewish ghetto in Poland was established at Lodz in April 1940.

★★★★★

The first British offensive in southeast Asia was in Burma on September 21, 1942.

★★★★★

The first U.S. mainland location to come under enemy fire was the oil fields west of Santa Barbara, Calif., by a Japanese submarine on February 24, 1942.

★★★★★

The first assault on a mainland U.S. military base by a foreign power was a Japanese submarine attack against Fort Stevens, Oreg., June 22, 1942.

★★★★★

The first combat action of the U.S. 36th Infantry Division was at Salerno, Italy. The 36th was the Texas National Guard.

★★★★★

The first person executed by the British for treason was George T. Armstrong, a sailor in the Royal Navy, who passed information to the Germans via their consul in New York. Captured by the FBI, Armstrong was turned over to the British, who hung him on July 9, 1941.

★★★★★

The first member of the Vichy French government to be tried and found guilty of collaboration with the enemy was former minister of the interior Pierre Pucheau. He was tried by a military court in Algiers in 1944 and sentenced to death.

The beaches of Anzio were "the largest self-supporting prisoner-of-war camp in the world" according to propaganda from Axis Sally (Mildred E. Gillars). Her radio broadcast reference chided the Allies' inability to break out from the beaches for a considerable time after the invasion.

★★★★★

The "Most Feared Man in Europe" was not Adolf Hitler but rather German supercommando Otto Skorzeny. He earned the title as a result of several daring events, including the November 12, 1943, rescue of Italian dictator Benito Mussolini. Skorzeny and a force of 90 men landed in the Abruzzi Mountains by glider and overwhelmed the garrison of 250 men guarding Mussolini. Skorzeny had also kidnapped the son of Hungarian dictator Admiral Miklos Horthy for Hitler in order to guarantee Hungary's support of Nazi goals. At various times Skorzeny was known to be working on plans for other kidnappings Hitler wanted: Pétain of France and Tito of Yugoslavia.

★★★★★

The quickest way for military personnel to send or receive a letter during the war was V-mail. It consisted of a special form that was microfilmed and reconstructed at the receiving end. Enlisted-personnel mail was subject to censorship whereas communications sent by officers were only spot-checked, as officers were relied on to observe security restrictions.

★★★★★

The first American to land in France during the Normandy invasion was Private Frank L. Lillyman, a pathfinder with the 101st Airborne Division. More than 1,600 U.S. aircraft and 512 gliders plus 733 British aircraft and 355 gliders dropped one British and two U.S. airborne divisions into France before the seaborne invasion began.

The first U.S. soldier to land in France was Army Corporal Frank M. Koons, an American Ranger who participated in the August 19, 1942, raid on Dieppe, France (Operation Jubilee). The mission was never intended to be a full-scale invasion but rather an effort to test the vulnerability of Hitler's fabled "Atlantic Wall." The assault included transport across the English Channel by Royal Navy ships and air cover by the RAF. Because the raid was to be a surprise, there was no advance naval or air bombardment. In terms of personnel, 5,000 troops of the 2nd Canadian Division were accompanied by 1,000 British Commandos and 50 American Rangers. Dieppe was a total failure. More than half of the 6,050 troops who landed were killed, captured, or wounded. The RAF lost more than 100 planes before the mini-invasion was called off and the Allies withdrew.

—U.S. Army photo

The first entire division to receive a Presidential Unit citation was the 101st Airborne. The photo above was taken during the official presentation and review on March 15, 1945, in France. In the rear of the jeep are Generals Dwight D. Eisenhower, Supreme Allied Commander, and Maxwell D. Taylor, commander of the division. Deputy Division Commanding Brigadier General G. J. Higgins is in the front with the unidentified driver. (NOTE: The photo negative was "flopped" during official processing, causing the steering wheel to be on the wrong side and the jeep's identification numbers to be backward.)
—U.S. Army photo

General Omar Bradley did not receive his first field command until after the U.S. entered the war in 1941. Bradley, like Eisenhower, was a member of the West Point class of 1915, known as "the Class the Stars Fell On" because its 164 graduates produced more generals (64) than any West Point class before or since. At the outbreak of war in Europe Eisenhower was a lieutenant colonel on the staff of General Douglas MacArthur in the Philippines. By the time the Japanese attacked Pearl Harbor, Eisenhower was a tank regiment commander under General George S. Patton. Prior to his first assignment to London during the war, Ike had been to Europe only once previously, to write a guidebook on American war monuments. Eisenhower rose from lieutenant colonel to general in less than 18 months. Eisenhower (left) and Bradley (right) flank Major General Louis A. Craig, commander of the 9th Division, during a November 8, 1944, meeting in Bütgenbach, Belgium.

—U.S. Army photo

The German army was better equipped as late as 1944 than it had been when the Nazis invaded Russia in 1941. This was generally credited to the efforts of Armaments Minister Albert Speer (left). He is seen in this photo shortly after the German surrender in May 1945 with Hitler's successor, Admiral Karl Doenitz, and General Alfred Jodl, chief of operations at OKW and Hitler's personal chief of staff. Speer and Doenitz were sentenced to prison terms at the Nuremberg trials. Jodl was hanged.

—U.S. Army photo

Eric Sevareid

Douglas Edwards

Edward R. Murrow

—All photos courtesy of CBS

Richard C. Hottelet

Charles Collingwood

The first marathon news broadcast on radio was the CBS News coverage of D-Day. The continuous reports were the result of months of planning for invasion coverage by Edward R. Murrow and his staff. Within a few short years television would make their faces as familiar as their voices had become on radio. Richard Hottelet was the first to report the seaborne invasion of Normandy and flew with the first wave of Maurauder bombers (9th Air Force) over France. He was aboard the plane that dropped the first bomb on Utah Beach six minutes before H-Hour. Charles Collingwood, using early recording equipment, reported from an army LST during the invasion. In 1940 Eric Sevareid had been the first newsman to report that France was about to capitulate to the Germans and ask for an armistice. As D-Day began, Sevareid was in Italy, covering the fall of Rome to the Allies. Murrow and Charles Shaw were in the sealed pressroom at Supreme Allied Headquarters in London. Bill Shadel was aboard the cruiser USS *Tuscaloosa* off the invasion beaches. "Eisenhower had his plan," noted Douglas Edwards, "and we had ours."

★★★★★

The only newsman expelled by the Allies from the European theater of operations was Associated Press reporter Edward Kennedy. He had violated a Supreme Headquarters Allied Expeditionary Force (SHAEF) directive advising that the story of the German surrender at SHAEF headquarters in Reims, France, on May 7, not be released until the Germans signed it with the Soviets in Berlin on May 8. The delay, to include the Soviets, was considered necessary in view of Soviet suspicions that the Americans and British were trying to "grab" Europe. The official announcements of the surrender were to be made simultaneously on May 8 by Truman, Churchill, and Stalin at 9 A.M. Washington, 3 P.M. London, and 4 P.M. Moscow time. Kennedy jumped the gun and filed the story shortly after General Jodl and representatives of the German high command surrendered unconditionally at SHAEF headquarters on May 7.

The first U.S. correspondent to land on the Normandy beaches on D-Day was Warren H. Kennet, a military writer with the now defunct *Newark News* (N.J.). He was also the only newsman present when the German 19th and 24th armies surrendered to New Jersey's 44th Infantry during the war.

★★★★★

The first American military personnel to enter Berlin were *Stars and Stripes* staffer Ernie Leiser and a soldier only identified as Mack Morris. They made the trip in April 1945, while the battle for the capital was raging.

★★★★★

The first U.S. combat troops to see action in Asia were members of the 5307th Composite Group, more commonly known as Merrill's Marauders. The nickname was created by newsman Jim Shepley of Time-Life, Inc.

★★★★★

Hitler arrived at his bunker under the Reich chancellery in Berlin for the last time on January 16, 1945. He remained there for the rest of the war, and his life.

★★★★★

The last person to see Adolf Hitler and Eva Braun alive was his valet, Heinz Linge.

★★★★★

The first enlisted member of the U.S. armed forces to receive a Medal of Honor in the war was USMC Sergeant John Basilone of Raritan Township, N.J. Basilone was given the medal on October 24, 1942, for heroism earlier that year during the battle for Guadalcanal. He was killed on Iwo Jima on February 19, 1945.

Carpet bombing was employed for the first time during the breakout at St.-Lô after the Normandy landings. However, more than 100 troops of the 30th Division and Lieutenant General Lesley J. McNair, an observer, were killed when a portion of the 5,000 tons of explosives fell on U.S. troops by mistake. The devastation inflicted on St.-Lô is obvious in this July 28, 1944, photo.

—U.S. Army photo

44

When the British Eighth Army under Lieutenant General Bernard Law Montgomery came up against Rommel's forces in October 1942 during the Second Battle of El Alamein, the British had more than 1,000 pieces of artillery, twice as much firepower as the Germans. Monty, left, is seen here a month later talking with captured General Ritter von Thoma after the British drove the Germans out of Egypt. Von Thoma had been second in command to Rommel.

—U.S. Army photo

The first, if premature, news about the liberation of Paris was the result of a mistake. And it was carried throughout the world. Charles Collingwood of CBS News had tape-recorded the story in advance and forwarded it to London for use at the appropriate time. However, a mixup resulted in its being broadcast on August 23, 1944, two full days before the actual liberation. This group of Parisians are seen reading one of the several liberation newspapers that sprang up when the 2nd French Armored of the 1st U.S. Army made it official.
—U.S. Army photo

The last German commander of Paris was General Dietrich von Choltitz, who disobeyed Hitler's orders to burn the city and instead surrendered it to the Allies in August 1944. As a colonel von Choltitz had been the first German officer to land in Holland and the Low Countries when the invasion started on May 10, 1940. Von Choltitz is seen here being interviewed by U.S. Army Major Sterling H. Abernathy shortly after the liberation of Paris.

—U.S. Army photo

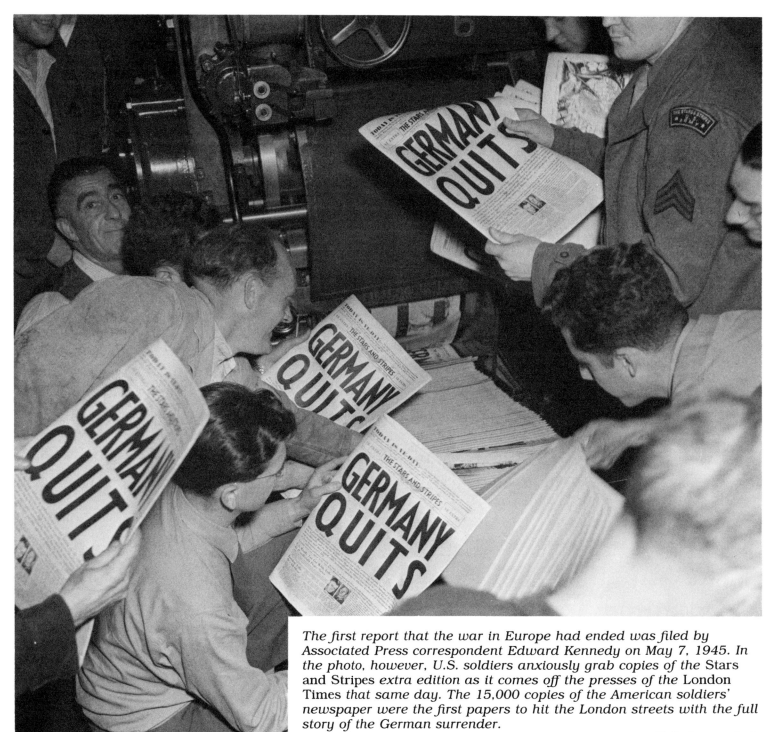

The first report that the war in Europe had ended was filed by Associated Press correspondent Edward Kennedy on May 7, 1945. In the photo, however, U.S. soldiers anxiously grab copies of the Stars and Stripes *extra edition as it comes off the presses of the* London Times *that same day. The 15,000 copies of the American soldiers' newspaper were the first papers to hit the London streets with the full story of the German surrender.*

—*U.S. Army photo*

The first stand-up land fight between the U.S. and the Japanese was at the Tenarru River on Guadalcanal. The August 7, 1942, invasion of Guadalcanal in the Solomon Islands was the first major U.S. land offensive in the war. The 1st Marine Division received naval and air support as it assaulted beaches on Guadalcanal (and four other islands in the Solomons). Initially, the 11,000 Marines faced no opposition as they came ashore. However, stiff resistance soon followed, causing the campaign to secure the island to last for six months.

★★★★★

The only three countries in the Atlantic occupied by U.S. Marines were Iceland, Trinidad, and British Guiana. On July 7, 1941, five months before its neutrality was to end abruptly, the U.S. sent the Marines there in order to free British troops for service elsewhere.

★★★★★

The only British territory occupied by Germany during the war was the nine Channel Islands, 80 miles south of the English coast and 40 miles from Cherbourg, France. They were invaded and occupied on June 30, 1940. The German garrison there surrendered on May 9, 1945.

★★★★★

The first Allied land victory of the war was at Narvik, Norway, on May 28, 1940, when the French Foreign Legion captured the port from the Germans.

★★★★★

The last train out of Paris carrying people to the Nazi concentration camps at Ravensbruk and Buchenwald departed on August 18, 1944, less than a week before the City of Light's liberation. Just under 300 of the approximately 2,450 people moved survived the war.

The largest single campaign, with regard to scope and the number of troops involved, was Operation Barbarossa in June 1941. Germany alone committed 300 divisions to it. In addition, Italian, Spanish, Hungarian, Slovakian, and Rumanian divisions moved against the Soviet Union with the Germans.

★★★★★

The closest the Germans got to Moscow after the June 1941 invasion of the Soviet Union (Operation Barbarossa) was within 25 miles. The units involved were the 3rd and 4th Panzer groups.

★★★★★

The first battle in which Japan had to defend territory the Empire had held prior to its conquests in the Pacific was Kwajalein (Operation Flintlock) in the Marshall Islands in January and February 1944. The Japanese were in the process of constructing an airstrip for bombers on boomerang-shaped Kwajalein Island itself at the southeast corner of the atoll. Consisting of a string of 100 islands and inlets, it is the largest coral atoll in the world. Kwajalein's land masses surround an irregularly shaped lagoon measuring 18 to 20 miles wide in places and approximately 70 miles long.

★★★★★

The first U.S. officer to be awarded the Medal of Honor in the war was U.S. Army Lieutenant Alexander R. Nininger, Jr., for action on Luzon in the Philippines on January 12, 1942, near Abucay, Bataan. It was awarded posthumously. The subsequent Japanese victory in the Philippines resulted in the greatest U.S. surrender in history (35,000 American and Filipino troops).

★★★★★

The first British land victory against the Japanese was at Sinzweza, Burma, on February 23, 1944.

THE AIR WAR

The only bombing of the United States mainland by enemy aircraft was accomplished by Japanese navy Lieutenant Nobuo Fujita on September 9, 1942. Launched by catapult from the submarine I-25 and flying a Yokosuka E14Y1, code-named Glen by the Allies, Fujita dropped four 167.5-pound phosphorus bombs on Mt. Emily along the timber coast in Oregon.

★★★★★

The first U.S. air attack against Japanese positions was the February 1, 1942, raid on the Marshall and Gilbert islands. The U.S. force, which included the aircraft carriers USS Yorktown (CV-5) and USS Enterprise (CV-6), five cruisers, and 10 destroyers, was the largest offensive since the outbreak of the war. Wake Island was included in the original planning. However, lacking aircraft support from the USS Lexington (CV-2) because of refueling problems, Wake was omitted.

★★★★★

Wake Island was where U.S. Marine pilots shot down their first Japanese planes and Okinawa was the last. Between those battles, USMC pilots scored 2,355 victories that resulted in 121 aces, including five pilots who scored 20 or more. In the Okinawa campaign alone Japan lost more than 7,800 aircraft, many of which were kamikazes. The U.S. lost approximately 800 planes.

★★★★★

Luftwaffe Major Erich Hartmann, with 352 victories, was known as "the Ace of Aces" of all nations. By the end of the war 36 German pilots recorded more than 100 kills, and five had more than 250. In addition to obvious ability there were two other reasons for their high scores: the Germans did not rotate tours of duty with rest periods as the Allies did, and they included ground targets as well as aircraft in their kill counts.

The first U.S. pilot to become an ace in two wars was A. J. Baumler, who scored eight kills during the Spanish Civil War and five kills in the China-Burma-India theater of operations during World War II.

★★★★★

The first pilot to land on the captured airfield on Iwo Jima was Lieutenant Raymond Malo, who brought his B-29, Dinah Might, in for an emergency landing on March 4, 1945, while the battle for the island was still in progress. By the end of the war more than 2,400 U.S. planes would land on the island.

★★★★★

The most decorated bomber pilot in the Luftwaffe was Obersleutnant (Lieutenant Colonel) Werner Baumbach, who at one time was the commander of the dreaded Kampfgeschwader 200 (KG 200), the Luftwaffe organization that flew U.S., British, and Soviet aircraft that had been captured or rebuilt after being shot down. This extremely secret group penetrated Allied airspace with crews who spoke the appropriate language, wore the correct uniforms, and passed themselves off as Allied fliers. They deposited spies on foreign soil, did photoreconnaissance, and attacked Allied units that they had attached themselves to (usually on return legs of bombing missions over Europe). There were no fewer than 48 KG 200 bases operating out of 11 countries.

★★★★★

The only U.S. Army Air Force pilot to defect to Germany was Lieutenant Martin J. Monti, who crossed sides in October 1944 by flying his fighter into Vienna and announcing that he wanted to fight against the Soviets. He was accepted, but rather than letting him join the Luftwaffe, the Nazis gave him command of an SS unit that was made up largely of Americans. After the war Monti was tried for treason and given a 25-year prison sentence.

The first B-29 raid on Japan did not occur until June 15, 1944, when 221 tons of bombs were dropped on the steel- and ironworks in Kyushu. This was the first attack on Japan itself since Doolittle's bold attack some two years earlier. Using a base in China, it was also the first air raid by U.S. land-based aircraft. The top photo graphically shows the havoc wreaked by B-29 incendiaries on Japan. The scene is the August 1, 1945, night raid on the aluminum-producing city of Toyama, which resulted in 95.6 percent destruction according to U.S. estimates. In the bottom photo a trio of B-29s pass Mt. Fujiyama en route to bombing Japanese targets.
—U.S. Air Force photos

It wasn't until November 24, 1944, that B-29s bombed Tokyo for the first time. Using airfields on Saipan in the Marianas, 111 planes participated. *Dauntless Dottie,* under the command of Major General Emmet O'Donnell, Jr., is credited with dropping the first bomb from a land-based aircraft.

★★★★★

Six Japanese cities were destroyed, four days before the first atom bomb was dropped, by a single 855-plane B-29 raid on August 2, 1945, which dropped several tons of jellied gasoline and magnesium bombs.

★★★★★

The most destructive single bombing mission of the war took place on March 9–10, 1945, when 334 B-29s raided Tokyo and left 1.25 million people homeless. This single raid caused a greater loss of life and more damage than either of the atom bombs dropped on Hiroshima and Nagasaki. The March raid killed 83,000 people, whereas 70,000 died in Hiroshima and 20,000 perished at Nagasaki.

★★★★★

The first air combat between Luftwaffe and RAF planes was on September 20, 1939, over Aachen, Germany.

The last air raid of the war was on August 14, 1945, the same day Japan agreed to surrender unconditionally. U.S. B-29s bombed Kumagaya, Isesaki, and Akita, Japan. The following day, August 15, was declared VJ-Day by President Harry S Truman, though the actual signing of the surrender was not until September 2 aboard the battleship USS *Missouri* (BB-63) in Tokyo Bay.

★★★★★

Japan's most successful aircraft against the B-29 Superfortress was the Nakajima Ki4411, code-named Tojo by the Allies. These high-altitude army interceptor-fighters first entered service in 1942. In one engagement alone, on February 19, 1945, Tojos are credited with shooting down ten B-29s.

★★★★★

The Japanese torpedo bomber Nakajima B5N2, code-named Kate by the Allies, was the type of aircraft credited with sinking three U.S. aircraft carriers in the war: USS *Lexington* (CV-2), USS *Yorktown* (CV-5), and USS *Hornet* (CV-8). During the attack on Pearl Harbor 144 Kates participated. The Kate was considered the best carrier-borne torpedo aircraft in the world in 1941.

The first B-29s were sent to India in April 1944, but the first combat use of the 60-ton giants wasn't until June 5, 1944, against the railroad yards in Bangkok on June 5, 1944, one day before the Normandy invasion in Europe. No B-29s operated in the European theater.

—Boeing photo, courtesy of John Fry

The Chance Vought F4U-4 Corsair, though designed for the U.S. Navy, was first flown off the decks of aircraft carriers by the Royal Navy. Its design was the winning entry in a 1938 U.S. Navy design contest for a shipboard single-seat fighter. The Corsair's designers set a goal for themselves to build the fastest fighter in the world. Based on the Pratt & Whitney Double Wasp engine, the V166 B design was approved and a prototype tested in 1939. The Corsair was also flown by U.S. Marine squadrons from ground bases.

—Courtesy of John Fry

The most widely produced of the 40 variants of the British Spitfire fighter was the Mk.IX, of which 5,600 were produced out of a total of 20,334 Spitfires produced. The Mk.IX series entered service in July 1941 with 64 Squadron. The top photo is a Submarine spitfire. The only time a Spitfire flew within sight of the Statue of Liberty, center photo, was in 1990, when one of the few surviving aircraft visited the U.S. in commemoration of the 50th anniversary of the Battle of Britain. The bottom photo shows a Spitfire with American markings after a belly landing in the surf at Palermo, Italy.
—(1 & 2) Courtesy of Jaguar Motor Corporation
—(3) National Archives photo

In what was the largest air battle involving jet aircraft, 30 out of 50 Me-262 German fighters were shot out of the sky over and around Berlin on April 10, 1945, by 1,232 attacking B-17 and B-24 bombers and their P-51 Mustang escorts. Ten of the American bombers were lost.

★★★★★

The first plane to drop an 8,000-pound bomb on Germany was a British Halifax on April 10–11, 1942. The target was Essen.

★★★★★

The first German targets to be bombed by the RAF were the naval bases at Wilhelmshaven and Brunsbüttelkoog, on September 4, 1939. However, of the 29 Wellington and Blenheim bombers sortied for the mission, 10 failed to locate their targets and returned to England without dropping a single bomb; one plane mistakenly attacked the town of Esbjerg in Denmark, a neutral at the time, which was more than 100 miles away from their pilot target; and three of the British planes mistook Royal Navy ships in the sea below them for German ships and attacked. On realizing their error they aborted the mission and returned to base; of the 15 RAF planes that made it to the target, German antiaircraft fire shot seven of them down. Of the remaining eight planes, three dropped bombs that were direct hits on the battleship *Scheer*, but they turned out to be duds.

★★★★★

The first member of the U.S. Army Air Force to participate in the bombing of the three major Axis capitals was Sergeant Kurt Hermann. He served with both the 8th and 12th air forces in Europe and flew bombing missions on Berlin and Rome. In the Pacific he was assigned to B-29s that bombed Tokyo. Hermann was reported missing in action in the Pacific after flying more than 105 missions.

The only RAF fighter pilot awarded a Victoria Cross in 1940 during the Battle of Britain was Lieutenant James B. Nicholson. He was cited for attacking a German squadron while his own aircraft was burning badly. The award was made posthumously. Germany used more than 3,550 aircraft, of which 2,000 were bombers, in the Battle of Britain. At the start of the campaign the RAF had only 704 serviceable aircraft versus 2,686 for the Luftwaffe. Britain lost 915 planes versus 1,733 German aircraft shot down.

★★★★★

The first single-engine, low-wing fighter with retractable landing gear in World War II was the Polikarpov. It had originally been called the Rata when the Soviets introduced it in the Spanish Civil War.

The first fighter plane designed by the British for use off an aircraft carrier was the Fairey Fulmer in 1940.

The first all-metal fighter plane produced by Italy was the Fiat G-50.

The first monoplane fighter to operate from a U.S. aircraft carrier was the Brewster Buffalo.

The first monoplane fighter to operate from a Japanese aircraft carrier was the Mitsubishi A5M4, code-named Claude by the Allies. It entered service in 1937 and was withdrawn in 1942.

The first monoplane used by the RAF was the Avro Anson. It was also the first RAF plane to employ retractable landing gear.

★★★★★

In what still exists as a record for creating aircraft in an emergency, the Australians designed and built a prototype of the CA-12 Boomerang fighter plane in four weeks. Because of the difficulty in obtaining U.S. or British aircraft to fend off the Japanese, the Australians were forced to instantly create their own. A total of 250 Boomerang fighters were produced during the war.

Two studies of the German V-1, Hitler's "Reprisal Weapon," in flight. The top photo was snapped immediately after a V-1's takeoff in France whereas the bottom photo, showing flame from the tail, was taken moments before the bomb hit its target in London.
—Top photo, U.S. Army
—Bottom photo courtesy of Joseph Niechwiadowicz

*The first German V-1, the Luftwaffe's flying bomb, called
Vergeltungswaffe-1 ("Reprisal Weapon 1") by Hitler and Buzz bombs
by the Allies, hit London in June 1944. The target here was the
Picadilly section.*

           —U.S. Air Force photo

The V-1 was followed a short time later in the war by the larger V-2 rockets, the first of which fell on London on September 8, 1944. A prototype had been launched as early as 1933, but work on what would become the V-2 moved ahead rapidly once the rocket testing center at Pennemünde was established in 1938. The V-2 caused 2,754 British fatalities.
—U.S. Army photo

Of the 8,000-plus V-1 rockets launched against England, slightly over 2,300 hit London. These 25-feet-long unmanned missiles delivered one ton of explosives and were capable of flying to a maximum distance of 155 miles after launch. Hitler, bent on revenge against the English people, did not use the V-1 against the critical military objectives of Southampton or Portsmouth, where the supply lines to France were being fed. Instead he rained terror on the civilian population. V-1 raids are credited with causing 5,479 deaths and injuring another 15,934 people. Some sources put the death toll at 6,184. Property losses included more than 1 million homes, 95 hospitals, 149 schools, and 11 churches destroyed or damaged.

★★★★★

The only pilot to qualify as an ace with *four* air forces was Michael Gladych, a native of Warsaw, who was a fighter pilot for Poland, France, Britain, Finland, and the U.S. He scored at least five victories with all but the Finns.

★★★★★

The first naval aviation command to fight in both the North Africa and Pacific theaters was Fighting 26, a squadron of F4F Wildcat fighters based on the aircraft carrier USS *Sangamon* (CVE-26). After participating in Operation Torch on November 8, 1942, the carrier returned to Norfolk, VA briefly and by Christmas was involved in support operations during the Guadalcanal campaign in the Solomon Islands.

★★★★★

The first U.S. Navy or Marine Corps pilot to shoot down a Japanese Zero was Lieutenant (JG) Walter Haas of Fighting 42 Squadron in June 1942 while flying off the USS *Hornet* (CV-8). The kill was initially reported as a Type 96 fighter because of the confusion in enemy aircraft recognition at this stage of the war.

The last U.S. bombs dropped on Berlin were by the Eighth Air Force on April 21, 1945. In the four years and eight months between the first British attack on August 25, 1940, and the end of the war, British and American air forces would conduct 363 air raids against Berlin.

★★★★★

The only French bombing of Berlin occurred on June 7, 1940. By comparison, the Allies destroyed a 10 times larger area of Berlin than German and Italian planes destroyed in London. Approximately 52,000 Berliners, five times more than the fatalities in London, were killed.

★★★★★

The worst air raid on Paris came the day after liberation on August 26, 1944. Nearly 150 planes of the Luftwaffe bombed the city for 30 minutes, killing 213 people, injuring almost 1,000 others, and destroying 597 buildings.

★★★★★

The target of the most destructive RAF air raid of the war was the city of Hamburg, Germany, on the night of July 27–28, 1943. More than 750 aircraft dropped 2,400 tons of bombs, many of which were incendiaries, on the city. The resultant fire storms created winds of more than 150 miles per hour. Official records put the death toll at 20,000 and the injured at more than 60,000.

★★★★★

The first Japanese heavy bomber to have a tail gun turret was the Nakajima Ki-49-II, code-named Helen by the Allies. The first low-wing monoplane fighter used by Japan was the Nakajima Ki-27, code-named Nate by the Allies.

The first bombing raid on Japan was on its capital, Tokyo, and the cities of Kobe, Nagoya, and Osaka on April 18, 1942, just over four months after Pearl Harbor. Lieutenant Colonel Jimmy Doolittle led a squadron of 16 specially fitted U.S. Army B-25 Mitchell bombers from the decks of the aircraft carrier USS Hornet (CV-8). Some months after the raid Brigadier General James H. Doolittle and two of the Army Air Force engineer-gunners who took part in the historic flight got together to talk about their experiences. From left: Technical Sergeant Eldred V. Scott, Sergeant David J. Thatcher, and Doolittle.
—U.S. Army Air Force photo

One of Jimmy Doolittle's B-25s at the moment it began moving down the deck of the USS Hornet (CV-8) on its way to take part in the first U.S. air raid on Japan.

—U.S. Navy photo

The B-25 Mitchell was the most heavily armed aircraft in World War II. It carried a 75-mm gun in the nose together with eight fixed and four movable machine guns. (The B-25J had the "glasshouse" nose for the bomb aimer instead of the 75-mm gun and four nose machine guns.) Going into service shortly before the attack on Pearl Harbor, the B-25 became one of the most widely used bombers in the war, with its most famous mission being Doolittle's Raid on Tokyo.
—U.S. Air Force photo

The Doolittle Raid was the first time aircraft as large as B-25s had ever been launched from an aircraft carrier. Originally 20 planes were to be used, but the new carrier was unable to accommodate that many. In planning the mission it was determined that the planes would be launched from 500 miles off the Japanese coast and that none would be able to return to the carrier. Plans were made to land at safe airfields in China. However, Task Force 16, which also included the carrier *Enterprise* and four cruisers, was spotted by Japanese picket boats while still 650 miles from Japan, and the decision was made to launch immediately. Thirteen B-25s struck Tokyo, and three bombed other cities for psychological reasons. One plane landed in the USSR and the crew was interned. Crews from the other 15 planes crash-landed or bailed out over occupied China, resulting in five deaths. Eight fliers were captured by the Japanese. Three of them were executed, and one died in captivity. Out of the 80 U.S. crew members on the mission 71 survived.

★★★★★

The first joint RAF and Soviet air raid against Germany was on April 16, 1945, when planes from the two countries attacked a train on the outskirts of Dresden.

★★★★★

The first time U.S. personnel participated as full crews in a bombing mission over occupied Europe was on July 4, 1942, when six American bombers were part of an RAF flight that bombed Luftwaffe airfields in Holland. The U.S. lost two aircraft in the action.

★★★★★

The first U.S. fighter squadron to shoot down 100 German planes was the *Avengers,* commanded by Francis S. (Gabby) Gabreski of Oil City, Pa. The *Avengers* were part of the Zemke group in the 8th Air Force and racked up the score in 86 days during the summer of 1943.

The only pilot to score 17 victories in a single day was Luftwaffe ace Jans J. Marseille. His eventual total reached 158. Not far behind, however, was Major Wilhelm Batz, also of the Luftwaffe, who racked up a triple ace score in 1942 when he had 15 victories against the Soviets in a single day. His total eventually reached 237 kills, ranking him sixth among German aces. Marseille was known as "the Star of Africa" by fellow pilots. The last Luftwaffe action in North Africa was at Benghazi on February 21, 1941.

★★★★★

The first combat mission of the U.S. Eighth Air Force was on August 17, 1942, from bases in England against the French railroad center in Rouen. The raid, which was led by General Ira Eaker, marked the first time U.S. piloted aircraft conducted a bombing mission without other Allies in the European theater of operations. RAF Spitfires, however, provided fighter protection for the U.S. bombers.

★★★★★

The first German aircraft shot down in the war was a Junkers 87 Stuka during the invasion of Poland on September 1, 1939. Polish air force fighter pilot Wladyslaw Gnys is credited with the kill. He became a member of the RAF after fleeing from Poland.

★★★★★

The first British plane shot down was a Wellington bomber on September 7, 1939, while on a bombing mission to destroy the German battle cruiser *Gneisenau.*

★★★★★

The first British civilian casualties as a result of a German air raid were in the Orkney Islands on March 16, 1940.

The P-47 Thunderbolt was the largest and heaviest single-seat propeller-driven fighter of World War II. Nicknamed the Flying Jug, the Thunderbolt entered active service in April 1943 and by the end of the war Republic Aviation had produced some 15,683, making it the most numerous of all U.S. fighter types in the war. Shown here are a pair of P-47N models.

—Courtesy of John Fry

*The top U.S. P-51 Mustang fighter ace was Major George Preddy with
26 victories, seen here in his plane* Cripes A'Mighty 3rd. *The original
name for the Mustang series of fighters was Apache.*
—*John Fry photo of painting by H. F. Copic*

The last B-17 Flying Fortress was produced at Boeing's Seattle, Wash., plant on April 9, 1945. The prototype had first flown in 1935 and astonished aviation experts when it covered a distance of 2,000 miles at the then remarkable speed of 252 mph. The B-17 was the mainstay of the U.S. Air Force's daylight high-level bombing missions over Europe from 1942 onward.

—Boeing photo, courtesy of John Fry

The last major Luftwaffe air raid of the war was the January 1, 1945, attack on Allied naval and air bases in the Low Countries and France. Of the 800 German planes that sortied, the Allies shot down 364 while losing 125.

★★★★★

The first German bombing of London occurred unintentionally on August 23, 1940. A navigational error caused 10 Luftwaffe bombers to miss their intended target (the oil storage dump at Thameshaven, east of the city) and drop their bombs on London itself. A number of old and historic buildings, including St. Giles Church, Cripplegate, were destroyed.

In retaliation, Berlin was bombed for the first time on August 25. The RAF selected industrial targets and sortied 81 aircraft across the English Channel: seven planes aborted before reaching Germany; 18 others were unable to locate Berlin and bombed alternate targets; 27 could not identify Berlin or any alternate targets. Only 29 planes actually bombed targets in Berlin, and five of them were shot down. The first RAF sorties over Berlin were on October 1, 1939, but instead of bombs the RAF dropped leaflets suggesting that the war Germany had started could have serious consequences for the Germans.

★★★★★

The first U.S. bombing of Berlin was by the Eighth Air Force on March 4, 1944. However, the first full-scale daylight raid on the city was March 6, when 814 U.S. bombers pounded the German capital. The last plane to return home from that mission was *Little Willie*, a B-17 of the 388th Bomb Group. Damaged over the target by flak and enemy aircraft, *Little Willie* turned for home, struggling all the way but unable to rise above 100 feet or exceed 115 miles per hour. Gravely damaged, the plane had been in the air nearly 10 hours before barely making it back to its base in England.

The first American pilot killed in action in the Pacific was U.S. Navy Ensign Manuel Gonzalez from the USS *Enterprise* on December 7, 1941.

★★★★★

The first B-17 pilot lost in combat was Captain Colin P. Kelly, Jr., on December 10, 1941. One of the most widely held pieces of misinformation concerning the war is that Kelly received a Congressional Medal of Honor for his actions following the sinking of the Japanese battleship *Haruna*. Kelly did not sink the battleship, nor did he receive the CMH. The *Haruna* was sunk by U.S. aircraft on Kure Island, Japan, on July 28, 1945. Kelly was awarded a posthumous Distinguished Service Cross for remaining in his aircraft while his B-17 crew bailed out. Saburo Sakai, Japan's third-highest scoring ace with 64 kills, is credited with shooting down Kelly's B-17.

★★★★★

The last air combat in the Pacific occurred over Japan on August 18, 1945, when the *Hobo Queen II*, a U.S. B-32 on photoreconnaissance, was engaged by Japanese fighters. One U.S. airman was killed and two others were wounded.

★★★★★

What is believed to have been the last bomb dropped on Japan during the war was released by U.S. Navy pilot John Wallace (Wally) McNabb of New Town, Pa. of bombing-fighting squadron of Air Group 87 aboard the USS *Ticonderoga* (CV-14). McNabb was the fourth man in the third four-man formation that was attacking Chosi Field near Tokyo on August 15, 1945. He was well into his dive on a target and was pushing the button to release a bomb when word was flashed over the radio that the Japanese has surrendered unconditionally. Air Group 87 was the senior naval air group in the Pacific when the war ended.

The largest planned crash landing by the USAAF during the war took place on July 15, 1942, when two B-17s and six P-38Fs were forced down on Greenland because of fake German weather reports that caused them to run low on fuel. At the top is a P-38 Lightning in flight. The first to land was Lieutenant Brad McManus, who took the bottom photo of Lieutenant Robert H. Wilson relaxing on his P-38F Lightning.
—Brad McManus photo courtesy of R. J. Reynolds Tobacco
—Lockheed P-38L photo courtesy of John Fry

Six P-38F Lightnings that were part of the largest intended crash landing in the war were the goal of an extraordinary recovery expedition sponsored by the R. J. Reynolds Tobacco Company in the 1980s. One had landed with its gear down and promptly flipped. The other five had skidded down with their gear up, preventing eventual takeoffs. The planes had been on their way to Great Britain from Maine, but the crews spent the next 10 days on an ice cap before being rescued just 45 miles from the Arctic Circle. Still there, the planes are believed to be under 35 to 40 feet of snow. No effort was made to recover the two B-17s that were also part of the flight. If successful, the recovery would have more than doubled the number of P-38Fs left in the world. Of the 9,600 made only five exist today.

★★★★★

The first, and most likely the only, airfield cleared of snow and made flight ready by a herd of reindeer was at Vaernes near Trondheim in central Norway. With almost no fuel left, more than two feet of snow on the airfield, and the German army closing in on their base, Norwegian air force pilots didn't feel their prospects of avoiding capture were very good. Suddenly, seemingly out of nowhere, a herdsman moving approximately 3,000 reindeer from the valley to the mountains appeared. After a brief negotiation in which the base medical officer provided the herdsman with a generous supply of alcohol for medicinal purposes, the herdsman and pilots stampeded the reindeer back and forth across an area large enough to permit takeoffs. The resultant pounding created a flat, hardpacked surface that was deemed satisfactory.

★★★★★

The first saturation bombing raid on Germany, involving 1,130 planes, was by the RAF on Cologne on May 30–32, 1942. The RAF air armada sortied from 52 airfields in Britain. In total Britain dropped just over 645,920 tons of bombs on Germany during the war.

The first American pilot believed to have deliberately crashed his plane into an enemy ship was U.S. Marine Corps Captain Richard E. Fleming, during the Battle of Midway. Fleming, his aircraft burning after being hit by antiaircraft fire, aimed and crashed on the deck of the Japanese cruiser Mikuma on June 6. He received a Medal of Honor posthumously. The Mikuma was sunk at Midway.

★★★★★

The last air combat in the European theater of operations was between an unarmed U.S. Piper Cub spotting plane named Miss Me and a German Fieseler Storch, also a spotter plane, over Germany in April 1945. Lieutenant Duane Francies, the American pilot, and his observer, Lieutenant William Martin, dove on the Storch and emptied their .45 Colt sidearms. They followed the German plane to the ground and captured their two counterparts. It was the only German plane reported to have been shot down with handguns.

★★★★★

The last strategic bombing of Germany involving large RAF formations was against Pilsen, Munich, Kiel, and Wangerooge on April 25, 1945.

★★★★★

The first Luftwaffe action in North Africa was against the British at Benghazi on February 12, 1941.

★★★★★

The first helicopter rescue ever was in the China-Burma-India theater of operations in April 1945, when U.S. Army Air Force Captain James L. Green was plucked out of the mountainous Burmese jungle. Green had crashed while himself on a search and rescue mission for downed pilots. Seriously injured, he was lifted to safety a week later by Lieutenant R. F. Murdock, flying a Sikorsky YR-4.

Josef (Pips) Priller and Heinz Wodarczyk were the only two Luftwaffe pilots to sortie and engage Allied forces during the D-Day invasion.
—U.S. Air Force photo

Marine fighter ace Joe Foss, a Medal of Honor recipient for action over Guadalcanal, was the first U.S. pilot in World War II to equal the 26 victories of World War I ace Captain Eddie Rickenbacker. "Swivel Neck Joe," flying a Grumman F4F-4 Wildcat, rang up his score in five months. Grumman and Eastern Aircraft built a total of 7,251 Wildcats. Of the fewer than 20 that have survived to the present, three are Grummans.

—Photo of painting by Lou Maniero

Of the 14 types of British fighters and bombers that saw service in the war, the Hawker Hurricane was the RAF aircraft type that sustained the greatest number of losses. First flown in 1935, a total of 14,231 had entered service by the end of the war. With approximately 60 percent of Fighter Command's squadrons flying Hurricanes, the aircraft was dubbed the workhorse of the Battle of Britain. The photo below shows one of the survivors still in flying condition in 1990.
—Courtesy of Jaguar Motor Corporation

The first U.S. pilots to operate from Japanese soil were members of Marine Aviation Group 31, who began flying from Yokosuka on September 7, 1945, five days after the surrender was signed. No U.S. aircraft operated from Japanese homeland bases during hostilities.

★★★★★

The island of Malta was known during the was as the "Most Bombed Spot on Earth" and became the first geographic area to be awarded a medal. After the fall of Greece and Crete and the introduction of the Afrika Korps in North Africa, the island of Malta became a significant naval and air base. The Germans saw the British colony as a threat to their supply lines and bombed the island almost continuously from January 1941 until the German defeat in North Africa in May 1943. Malta received the George Cross from Britain for its heroic stand.

★★★★★

The top French air ace of the war was Marcel Albert, with 23 kills. Svein Heglund, with 15 victories, was Norway's top ace, although he racked up his score while flying with the RAF.

★★★★★

The best French fighter in the war was the Dewoitine D-520. France only had 36 of them in service before the armistice with Germany. Under occupation approximately 870 were produced for use by the Luftwaffe and the Italians, Bulgarians, and Rumanians.

★★★★★

The first sinking by aircraft of a major combat vessel was the April 10, 1940, German loss of the cruiser *Königsberg* as a result of bombing by RAF Blackburn Skuas while the ship was dockside in Bergen Harbor.

The most successful jet pilot of the war was Lieutenant Colonel Heinz Bar, who ranked ninth overall among Germany's aces. Bar, who himself was shot down 18 times, racked up 220 kills, 16 of which were while flying the Me-262 jet.

★★★★★

The greatest number of sorties flown by any pilot in the war was 2,530 by Luftwaffe fighter ace Hans Ulrich Rudel. He is credited with destroying more than 500 enemy tanks. He is the only German ever awarded a Knight's Cross to the Iron Cross with Golden Oak Leaves and Swords and Diamonds. On its institution, it became the second-highest degree of the Iron Cross (the highest degree was the Great Cross of the Iron Cross, which was also only awarded once: to Hermann Goering).

★★★★★

In total the RAF flew 687,462 bombing missions and dropped more than 1,103,900 tons of bombs on all fronts during the war.

★★★★★

The first air battle between the RAF and the Luftwaffe occurred over the German city of Aachen on September 20, 1939. A flight of Messerschmitt 109s engaged a trio of British Battles that were patrolling in the vicinity of the French-German border. Britain lost two aircraft versus one for the Luftwaffe.

★★★★★

The only Allied pilots attached to the Soviet air force as a unit were a Free French fighter group named Normandie. They functioned from early 1943 on with the First Soviet Air Division. Four members received the USSR's highest decoration: Hero of the Soviet Union for scoring more than 10 kills.

Prior to the invasion of North Africa (Operation Torch), Vichy French Algiers had little to worry about from Allied air raids. Once it was occupied, however, the city's extensive antiaircraft defenses and searchlights were frequently in use to deter German planes.
—*Courtesy of Mrs. Robert Goralski*

The first air raid alarm to sound in Britain occurred on September 6, 1939, five days after the war began in Europe. It turned out to be a tragic false alarm, however, in which RAF Spitfires mistakenly shot down two RAF Hurricanes. Once the Battle of Britain began, however, Londoners took to spending their nights in the Underground as German bombs rocked the streets above them.

—*Courtesy of Mrs. Robert Goralski*

The first American pilot to become an ace by scoring five victories in one day was Robert (Duke) Hedman, a volunteer with the Flying Tigers. He accomplished the record on December 25, 1941.
—Painting by artist Lou Maniero

The first combat action by the Flying Tigers against the Japanese was on December 20, 1941, 13 days after Pearl Harbor, over Kunming, China. The highest-scoring ace in the Flying Tigers was Robert Neale, who scored 16 victories while a member. The Americans in General Claire Chennault's volunteer group were paid $600 per month plus $500 for each Japanese plane shot down. Formed in 1941 under the cover name Central Aircraft Manufacturing Company, their actual purpose was to fight the Japanese for China. The fighting units were called the American Volunteer Group when they began training in September. After the attack on Pearl Harbor they became the U.S. Fourteenth Air Force but were better known as the Flying Tigers. They were the first American pilots to use rockets in air combat in the Pacific.

★★★★★

The first U.S. pilot to shoot down four Japanese planes in one day was Lieutenant George S. Welch, assistant operations officer of the 47th Pursuit Squadron based at Wheeler Field, Oahu, Hawaii, on December 7, 1941. Welch and another officer, Lieutenant Kenneth M. Taylor, piloted two P-40 fighters from Haleiwa Field, a makeshift airfield used for short-field practice landings, to Wheeler to get fuel and .50-caliber ammunition.

★★★★★

The first regular U.S. armed forces pilot to become an ace by scoring five victories in a single day was Navy Lieutenant Edward (Butch) O'Hare, on February 20, 1942. O'Hare, who flew off the USS *Lexington* (CV-2), shot down five Japanese bombers in five minutes. The action resulted in his receiving the Medal of Honor. O'Hare was killed in action by friendly fire while stationed on the USS *Enterprise* (CV-6) in the central Pacific in 1944. His aircraft was mistaken as Japanese by the rear gunner of a TBF during a night mission. Chicago's O'Hare International Airport was named in his honor.

The first fighter pilot to score more than 100 victories was Lieutenant Werner Molders of the Luftwaffe. He was also the first pilot to be decorated with the Knight's Cross with Oak Leaves, Swords, and Diamonds (Germany's highest award). Molders, enroute to funeral services for General Ernst Udet in November 1941, was one of several passengers killed in a plane crash.

★★★★★

The first five U.S. Army Air Force sergeants to fly in combat as pilots, despite regulations that only commissioned officers could serve as pilots, were John Ferguson, Bayside, N.Y; Dennis L. A. Johns, Jackson, Mich.; Daniel L. Richards, Long Beach, Calif.; Donald E. Dempsey, Elyria, Ohio; and William C. Aney, Buffalo, N.Y. They had flown Spitfires for the Royal Canadian Air Force since 1941. When they transferred to the U.S., they were already seasoned pilots. All first saw action for the U.S. flying Mustangs against the Luftwaffe in the European theater during 1944.

★★★★★

The largest contingent of foreign pilots in the Royal Air Force were the Canadians. Canada had 42 squadrons among the 487 in the RAF by the time the Allies invaded France. Yugoslavia had one squadron. In all there were 157 international squadrons in the RAF by D-Day.

★★★★★

The first American pilot to fly alone and unarmed over Berlin was Major Walter L. Weitner, who did photoreconnaissance on March 6, 1944.

★★★★★

The greatest number of planes shot down in a single day by an American pilot was nine on October 24, 1944, by U.S. Navy pilot David McCampbell.

Japanese suicide pilots didn't limit their deadly attacks only to ships. This unusual shot of a C-47 shows the damage caused by a frustrated kamikaze pilot who deliberately crashed into the transport when he was unable to bring it down with gunfire. But as the photo proves, the pilot was nonetheless able to return to base.

—McDonnell Douglas photo

The largest number of aircraft lost by the RAF since the start of hostilities occurred on May 14, 1940, when German defenders at Sedan shot down 45 Blenheims and Battles out of a 109-plane attacking force.

★★★★★

The Gloster Gladiator was the last series of single-seat biplane fighters used by the RAF in the war. Flown for the first time in 1934 and ordered in quantity by the RAF in 1935, the Gladiator was actually a continued development of the earlier Gauntlet. The biplane, however, was already obsolete by the time two RAF squadrons, numbers 72 and 73, were outfitted with them before hostilities broke out in Europe. The RAF eventually took possession of 767 Gladiators. Gladiators were also in service with China, Sweden, and Finland.

★★★★★

The last of 2,392 Fairey Swordfish biplane bombers was delivered to the RAF on August 18, 1944. The first had been delivered in 1936. At their high point no less than 26 RAF squadrons had Swordfish among their numbers. It had been Swordfish that conducted the attack against the Italian naval base at Taranto in 1940 and led the air attack on *Sharnhorst, Gneisenau,* and *Prinz Eugen.* A Swordfish had also been involved in the sinking of the *Bismarck.*

★★★★★

The first Allied victory against a German plane was made by a U.S.-built Lockhead A-29 Hudson in service with the British Coastal Command. A Hudson was also the first American plane credited with sinking a German U-boat.

★★★★★

The first U.S. Army Air Force aircraft to see action in Europe was the Douglas A-20G Havoc on July 4, 1942.

The most planes ever shot down by a pilot on his first mission was seven, by Captain William A. Shomo, who received the Medal of Honor for the January 11, 1945, feat over Luzon in the Philippines. Shomo and another plane on photoreconnaissance encountered a Japanese twin-engine bomber and 12 fighter escorts. Shomo maneuvered and attacked several times, shooting down six fighters and the bomber; the other plane shot down three more fighters; and the remaining trio escaped in a cloud bank. In civilian life Shomo was a mortician.

★★★★★

In a dogfight between pilots who would each become his country's second-highest-scoring aces, Japan's Shoichi Sugita with 80 victories shot down Thomas B. McGuire, Jr., of the U.S., who had 38 kills. In some records Sugita is credited with as many as 120 kills.

★★★★★

General George C. Kenny began his U.S. Army Air Force career as an enlisted man in World War I and is credited with having shot down Hermann Goering (who survived).

★★★★★

The highest casualty rate for U.S. Air Force personnel in the European theater of operations was for heavy-bomber crews. The odds were nine to one that they would become casualties. This was almost three times as great as the rate for medium-bomber crews and just under twice the rate sustained by fighter pilots.

★★★★★

Italy's top air ace in the war was Major Adriano Visconti, with 26 kills. Despite Italy's inferior air power due to lack of aircraft, its pilots were considered among the finest in the war.

Only 33 of the 178 U.S. B-24 Liberators that participated in the August 1, 1943, attack against the German-occupied oil refineries at Ploesti, Rumania, ever saw combat again. German fighters shot down or seriously damaged the other 145. The right photo shows a "box" of B-24s en route to the target. The remarkable photo below captures the instant of a flak burst as seen from the top turret of a Liberator from Group 456, Squad 646, Fifteenth Air Force, en route to Ploesti.
—Courtesy of Mrs. Kenneth L. Bougner

★★★★★

The best-preserved missing-in-action aircraft located after the war was a B-24 Liberator found in the Libyan desert in May 1959, 16 years after being reported overdue at her North African air base. *The Lady Be Good* and her crew of nine had participated in the successful bombing of Naples in April 1943 but because of a navigational error overshot the air base at Soluch, Libya, and instead made a relatively soft crash landing on a plateau some 440 miles deep in the desert when she ran out of fuel. An oil exploration team stumbled on the perfectly preserved bomber in an area where daytime temperatures reach 130 degrees Fahrenheit. From evidence found both at the site and in an exhaustive investigation that followed, it was determined that the crew survived the landing but perished while attempting to make their way to civilization.

★★★★★

The first American bomber shot down after bombing Italy was a B-24 Liberator named *Natchez to Mobile, Memphis to St. Jo* of 344th Squadron, 98th bombardment Group (Heavy), on December 11, 1942. The squadron was some miles out over the Mediterranean and returning to its base after completing a raid on Naples harbor when it was engaged by Italian fighters. The 98th was normally based at Kabrit, Egypt, near the Suez Canal, but this raid was staged from Landing Ground 139 in the Western Desert near Tobruk. Navigator David Westheimer and six other crew members survived and were taken prisoner.

★★★★★

The only Allied jet to see service in the war was Britain's Gloster Meteor, seen above, which joined the RAF in July 1944. The Meteor was primarily used to intercept and shoot down V-1 rockets. The propeller-driven British Hawker Tempest, a bomber-fighter, was also a successful V-1 hunter and is credited with intercepting and destroying more than 600 of them.

—U.S. Air Force photo

★★★★★

Germany was the only nation to fly jet aircraft in combat during the war. (Britain's Gloster Meteor was used only to intercept and shoot down German V-1 rockets.) The first jet fighter was the German Messerschmitt-262, which, after six years of development, made its maiden flight in July 1942 and shot down its first enemy plane, a De Havilland Mosquito, in July 1944. However, the Me-262, armed with 48 rockets, didn't enter squadron service until the end of 1944. The fighter version was the Me-262A-1a Schwalbe (Swallow), and the Me-262A-2a Sturmvogel (Stormbird) was adapted as a fighter-bomber. The fighter version had a top speed of 560 miles per hour and a range of 606 miles as opposed to the popular piston engine Messerschmitt-109G (400 miles per hour speed and 460 mile range). Though Germany produced 1,433 Me-262 jets, fewer than 200 of both types saw service in the war. Their performance left no doubt of what they were capable of doing. In one engagement alone six Me-262s shot down 14 B-17 Flying Fortresses.

★★★★★

The world's first jet aircraft was a Campini N-1, piloted by Marion de Bernardi, which flew between Milan and Rome on August 28, 1940. Italy did not fly any jets in the war.

★★★★★

World War II was the last war fought with aircraft using internal combustion engines.

The first U.S. jet plane flown during the war years was the Bell XP-59 on October 1, 1942, in California's Mojave Desert at Muroc, later Edwards Air Force Base. The first U.S. jet fighter, the Lockheed P-80 Shooting Star, flew for the first time on January 8, 1944 (but not in combat until June 1950 in Korea).

★★★★★

Germany also produced the only rocket-propulsion aircraft of the war, the Messerschmitt Komet, which made its debut on July 28, 1944. About 350 went into service, but more were destroyed in landing accidents than were shot down by the Allies.

★★★★★

The first aircraft built strictly as a jet-engined bomber of the war was also German, the Arado 234, nicknamed the Blitz. It was flown for the first time in 1944. In addition to being a four-engine tactical bomber, a two-engine version saw brief service as a high-altitude reconnaissance aircraft. Mounted with four 30-mm cannon and only two bombs (a one ton and a 1,000 pounder), the Blitz was capable of speeds of just over 490 miles per hour.

★★★★★

The first German bombs fell on Moscow on July 21, 1941, and the first Soviet bombs hit Berlin on August 8, 1941, but the Soviet mission was a failure. Five Soviet planes could do nothing more than bomb a section of railroad on the outskirts of the city. Two planes were downed by antiaircraft fire.

★★★★★

The first totally American bombing raid on Germany was on January 27, 1943, against the port facilities at Wilhemshaven.

The first British bombs fell on Italy during a night raid against Turin, June 11–12, 1940, by 36 Whitley bombers. However, only 10 planes actually dropped ordinance in the general target area: 10 planes hit the Fiat factory and alternate targets in Turin, two bombed Genoa, one plane was reported missing, and the remaining 23 had to abort because of bad weather.

★★★★★

The first Italian target hit during an RAF daylight raid was Milan on October 24, 1942. It wasn't until December 4, 1942, two and a half years after the Turin raid, that the first U.S. bombs, from B-24s, fell on Italy at Naples Harbor.

★★★★★

The first Italian heavy bomber was the Piaggio P-108 B, which entered service in 1942. It was notable for the installation of a remote-controlled gun in each of the outer-engine narcelles. In all it was armed with eight 12.7-mm guns and had a maximum bomb load of 7,716 pounds and a range of 2,500 miles.

★★★★★

Italy's last operational float plane was the Fiat RS-14. With a range of 1,553 miles, it had originally been designed as a land-based bomber but was adapted first for coast patrol and then for torpedo bombing. Its armament included one 12.7-mm and two 7.7-mm guns. The Fiat RS-14 carried 880 pounds of bombs or two 335-pound depth charges.

★★★★★

The only Italian plane to operate in combat in both the European and Pacific theaters was the Fiat Cicogna light bomber. Italian pilots flew them over Britain. In the Pacific it was the Japanese who flew them against China. Tokyo had purchased 75 Cicognas from Italy in 1938.

The first atom bomb was detonated on the ground in a test at 5:30 A.M. on July 16, 1945, in New Mexico. The first plane to drop an atom bomb on a populated area was the Enola Gay *on Hiroshima, Japan, August 6, 1945. The second, and last to date, was* Bock's Car *on Nagasaki (insert photo) on August 9, 1945. If it had become necessary to drop a third atom bomb, the target would have been Tokyo. On August 10, 1945, the day after Nagasaki, U.S. planes dropped counterfeit Japanese yen warning that a third bomb would be dropped unless Japan surrendered. The obverse of the bogus money was authentic looking while the reverse carried the third-bomb message. Tokyo was not mentioned as the target.*

—U.S. Air Force photos

58381

More than 5,000 women served as pilots in the Soviet air force. Lieutenant Lilya Litvak, with seven victories, and Lieutenant Katya Budanova, with six victories, were the two top female aces. Both piloted Yak-9 (Yakolov) fighters, which were particularly effective against German planes and tanks. Litvak was killed in action over the Eastern Front.

—U.S. Air Force photo

The only captured German plane used by the U.S. Army for scouting purposes was a brown Messerschmitt 109, which the 83rd Infantry Division repainted in traditional U.S. Army olive green.

★★★★★

The first U.S. pilot to shoot down a German plane after America entered the war was Army Air Corps Lieutenant Samuel F. Junkin on August 19, 1942, during the raid on Dieppe, France.

★★★★★

The only person aboard the B-25 Heckling Hare to be awarded the Silver Star for action over New Guinea when it was engaged by Japanese aircraft was Navy Lieutenant Commander Lyndon B. Johnson.

★★★★★

Henry H. (Hap) Arnold was the first five-star general in the Army Air Force. He had learned to fly from the Wright brothers and had been one of the first five pilots in the Army Air Corps.

★★★★★

The Luftwaffe, under the command of Reichsmarschall Hermann Goering, had the greatest number of Nazis in its ranks compared to the German army and navy.

★★★★★

The first U.S. Army Air Corps squadron made up totally of black American pilots was the 99th Pursuit Fighter Squadron, named the Lone Eagles.

★★★★★

The first German city to be hit by 4,000-pound bombs was Emden, during an RAF raid on March 31, 1941.

The total number of aircraft used by both sides during the war was approximately 675,000 planes, of which 475,000 were used by the Allies.

★★★★★

The U.S.-built Grumman F6F Hellcat made its combat debut on September 1, 1943, when Navy planes from the decks of the second aircraft carrier named USS *Yorktown* (CV-10) attacked Marcus Island, approximately 1,200 miles from Tokyo. The Hellcat saw service only in the Pacific theater.

★★★★★

The Japanese first introduced the kamikaze during the Battle for Leyte Gulf, October 23–26, 1944. The term means "divine wind" and refers to the great typhoon that struck and wiped out the invading Mongol fleet as it prepared to invade Japan during the Middle Ages.

★★★★★

The top U.S. ace of the war was Major Richard I. Bong, with 40 kills, of the Fifth Army Air Force. He led a squadron of P-38s named the Flying Knights.

★★★★★

The last aircraft to leave Dunkirk was a Westland Lysander nicknamed the Lizzie.

★★★★★

The last Allied bombing raid of the war in Europe occurred on May 2, 1945, when a squadron of RAF Mosquitoes attacked Kiel.

The most widely produced Japanese medium bomber was the Imperial Navy's Mitsubishi G4M1, code-named Betty by the Allies but nicknamed "the Flying Lighter" by U.S. pilots, who ignited more than a few of the 2,446 built. In the top photo a specially marked Betty (white, painted with green crosses) prepares to land at Ieshima on August 19, 1945, with Japanese envoys en route to Manila to discuss surrender formalities with General Douglas MacArthur's staff. In the right photo the envoys, replete with samurai swords and flowers, deplane. The journey from Ieshima to Manila was via a U.S. C-54.
—U.S. Navy photo

THE SEA WAR

The first battleship added to the U.S. fleet after war broke out in Europe was the 44,800-ton USS Washington *(BB-56),* launched on June 1, 1940. A scant 12 days later, however, the Washington *was joined by her sister ship, USS North Carolina (BB-55). Washington's massive, 108-foot beam can be appreciated in a head-on hull shot taken at the time of her launching in 1940.*

U.S.S. WASHINGTON

The USS *Washington* (BB-56), at 729 feet in length, became the largest battleship in the U.S. fleet at the time of her commissioning. At a White House meeting with President Roosevelt a year later (June 9, 1941), Admiral Husband E. Kimmel asked the President to send the *Washington* and her sister ship, *North Carolina* (BB-55), to join the fleet at Pearl Harbor. Roosevelt, however, decided to keep these big new ships in the Atlantic. With the commissioning of the first of the Iowa-class battleships on February 22, 1943, and before war's end, these two ships would be dwarfed by four larger U.S. battleships: *Iowa* (BB-61), *New Jersey* (BB-62), *Missouri* (BB-63), and *Wisconsin* (BB-64), all of which displaced 55,710 tons and were 887 feet long (which made them the longest battleships ever built by any nation). The heavyweights, in terms of displaced tons, were the Japanese sister battleships *Yamato* and *Musashi*, which came in at a gigantic 72,809 tons and were 862 feet long.

★★★★★

The only U.S. battleship to sink a Japanese battleship in the war was the 44,800-ton USS *Washington* (BB-56), which sank the 36,610-ton *Kirishima* on November 15, 1944, off Savo Island in the Solomons.

★★★★★

The first battleship sunk by dive-bombing planes was the USSR's *Marat* by German Stukas in the port of Kronstadt in September 1941. It was also the only Soviet battleship sunk in the war.

★★★★★

Only three crewmen out of the 1,421 aboard the HMS *Hood* survived the fatal engagement with the German battleship *Bismarck*.

★★★★★

The USS *Iowa* (BB-61) was known as the First Lady of the Third Fleet.

The USS *North Carolina* (BB-55) was the first U.S. battleship to see action after Pearl Harbor when it participated in the Battle of the Eastern Solomons on August 24, 1942.

★★★★★

The last battle between capital ships was on December 26, 1943, between the German battle cruiser *Scharnhorst* and the British battleship *Duke of York* in the Barents Sea. The *Scharnhorst* was hit by four torpedoes fired by Norwegian and British destroyers as she attempted to attack an Allied convoy bound for Murmansk, Russia. The *Duke of York*, three cruisers, and six destroyers then closed for a final, all-out attack, sinking the *Scharnhorst* less than 15 minutes later. Allied ships picked up 36 survivors from the crew of 1,900.

★★★★★

The last ship to leave France before capitulation in 1940 was the Polish passenger liner *Batory*, on June 22. Polish government officials and various officers and troops of the Polish army who had seen action in France departed from St.-Jean-de-Luz.

★★★★★

The first ship to return to France with the Normandy invasion fleet in June 1944 was the American destroyer USS *Corry*, under the command of Lieutenant Commander George D. Hoffman. It was the lead ship in the vanguard of Task Force O.

★★★★★

The first exchange of gunfire between U.S. and German ships was approximately 175 miles southwest of Iceland on September 4, 1941. The destroyer USS *Greer* had been tracking U-652, which turned and fired torpedoes. In exchange the American ship dropped depth charges. Neither side scored a hit.

USS Washington (BB-56) on the way to raid the Gilbert Islands in November 1943. (NOTE: The first battleship USS *Washington* [BB-47] was in the process of being built when the World War I ended. Never completed, it was expended as a target ship in naval gunnery practice.)

—*U.S. Navy photo*

94

The first ship sinking in the war occurred on September 1, 1939, the day Germany invaded Poland. The British passenger liner *Athenia,* with 1,400 people aboard, was torpedoed and sunk by *U–30* west of Scotland while en route to Canada. Twenty-eight Americans were among the 118 passengers killed in the attack. Although Berlin had issued specific orders that warnings be given to civilian ships, the commander of *U–30* failed to do so. Germany denied responsibility even after it later discovered that *U–30* had mistaken the *Athenia* for an armed merchant cruiser.

★★★★★

The first U.S. ship sunk after war began in Europe was the merchantman SS *City of Rayville,* which struck a mine in the Bass Strait off Cape Otway, Australia, on November 8, 1940. The minefield had been laid by the German raider *Pinguin,* one of 10 warships disguised as merchant ships.

The *Pinguin* became the first German raider sunk when its cargo of 130 mines exploded after being hit by eight-inch shells from the British cruiser *Cornwall* on May 8, 1941, in the Indian Ocean.

★★★★★

The last of the 10 armed German merchantmen to be sunk by the Allies was the *Michel.* It was torpedoed by the submarine USS *Tarpon* off Japan in October 1943. The merchantmen raiders accounted for 133 Allied ship sinkings, totaling 830,000 tons.

★★★★★

The first U.S. military casualties from hostile action came nearly two months *before* Pearl Harbor. Eleven sailors aboard the USS *Kearney* were killed when the destroyer was torpedoed while escorting a British convoy off Iceland.

That same day a U.S. merchantman, the *Lehigh,* was sunk by a German U-boat off the African coast.

The first U.S. military protection for U.S. merchant ship convoys in the North Atlantic, consisting of aircraft and destroyers, was not instituted until March 1, 1941.

★★★★★

The Royal Navy sustained the lowest number of British combat fatalities, 50,758 compared to the 69,606 lost by the Royal Air Force and the 144,079 army personnel reported killed or missing.

★★★★★

The U.S. placed the largest peacetime naval procurement order of all time on September 9, 1940, when it awarded contracts for 210 ships, including seven battleships and 12 aircraft carriers.

★★★★★

The first sinking of a U.S. Navy ship in 1941 occurred on October 31, 38 days *before* Pearl Harbor, when a German U-boat torpedoed the obsolete but seaworthy destroyer USS *Reuben James* off the west coast of Iceland. One hundred and fifteen men, including the captain and all officers, were lost. The *"Rube,"* in a clear violation of U.S. neutrality, was assisting British warships escorting a convoy of merchantmen from Halifax.

In a separate action the same day another U.S. Navy ship, USS *Salinas,* was also torpedoed in the North Atlantic off Newfoundland. However, the oiler sustained no casualties and was able to make port.

★★★★★

The first American casualty, other than Air Force, in the war in Europe was Lieutenant Colonel Loren B. Hillsinger, during the August 19, 1942, raid on Dieppe, France. He was aboard the destroyer *Berkley* and lost a leg when the ship was bombed by the Luftwaffe.

The first order authorizing U.S. Navy ships and planes to consider as hostile, and to attack, any Axis ships within 25 miles of the Western Hemisphere was issued on April 18, 1941, by Admiral Ernest J. King.
—U.S. Navy photo

On December 12, 1937, while Japan was at war with China but almost two years before war broke out in Europe, the U.S. Navy gunboat *Panay* and three ships belonging to an American oil company were bombed by aircraft while at anchor in the Yangtze River between Nanking and Wuhu, China. Four British gunboats also came under fire. Two sailors and a civilian were killed and 74 people were injured on the American ships. The clearly marked U.S. gunboat, which had entered service in 1928, came under attack from six Japanese aircraft at 1:38 P.M. The Japanese, who had been at war since invading China in 1931, apologized to both the U.S. and the British for the "mistake" and actually paid the U.S. more than $2.2 million in damages as a settlement of the *Panay* incident. However, less than two months after the attack on Pearl Harbor the Japanese government bestowed the Kinshi Kinsho Medal to Colonel Kingoro Hashimoto, the officer whom a U.S. Navy court of inquiry determined had given the order for the attack.

★★★★★

The greatest number of U-boats sunk on a single day by the Allies was seven, on July 7, 1944. These were, however, the German one-man submarines, called *Biber* (beaver). Slightly under 30 feet in length, the *Biber* U-boats were credited with sinking at least a dozen merchant vessels and nine navy ships.

★★★★★

Germany's most successful U-boat commander was Otto Kretschmer, who sank 45 ships during 16 patrols as commander of *U-23* and *U-99*. He was the first U-boat commander to sink more than a quarter-million tons of enemy shipping. On March 17, 1941, after an engagement with the destroyers HMS *Walker* and HMS *Vanoc*, Kretschmer and his crew were captured after scuttling their boat by Royal Navy Captain Donald Macintyre. Twenty percent of the German U-boat fleet was lost in March 1941 as a result of British air and naval fire. In addition to Kretschmer, the toll included several other veteran U-boat commanders.

More than half of the total Japanese merchant marine tonnage lost in the war was due to U.S. submarines, bringing Japan to the edge of starvation.

★★★★★

The destroyer escort USS *England* (DE-635) holds the record for sinking the greatest number of Japanese submarines in the shortest time period, five enemy subs in eight days during May 1944: *I-16*, May 19; *RO-106*, May 22; *RO-104*, May 23; *RO-116*, May 24; *RO-108*, May 26. The *England* extended that to six submarines in 12 days, also a record, when she sank *RO-105* on May 31. The *England*'s first kill of the series, a Japanese I-class submarine, was larger than the destroyer escort herself. The six submarines were part of a group of 25 the Japanese sent in advance of its fleet as scouts for what would become known as the Battle of the Philippine Sea. Seventeen were sunk.

★★★★★

The first member of the U.S. Submarine Service to receive the Medal of Honor (posthumously) was Commander Howard Gilmore of the USS *Growler* in 1943. Gilmore had ordered his officers to clear the bridge of the submarine while he remained on deck to maneuver the *Growler* to safety after it had rammed a Japanese gunboat. Injured in the exchange of gunfire that followed, Gilmore gave his last order to the officer of the deck: "Take her down." With her captain remaining topside, the *Growler* dived; it was seriously damaged but managed to escape to safety.

★★★★★

The first Japanese ship sunk by the U.S. after the attack on Pearl Harbor was the merchant ship *Atsutasan Maru*, by the submarine *Swordfish* on December 15, 1941.

The gunboat USS Panay (PR-5) was attacked and sunk by the Japanese in 1937, four years before the Pearl Harbor attack. This photo shows the Panay under steam a short time before the incident. In photo at right Commander E. R. Mahlmann and an unidentified sailor return Japanese aircraft fire during the attack.

—U.S. Navy photo

The first person to suggest the idea of a cross-channel invasion of England to Adolf Hitler was Grand Admiral Erich Raeder, commander in chief of the German navy, on May 21, 1940. Less than two months later Hitler authorized the actual planning of what became Operation Sea Lion. A veteran of World War I, Raeder rose through naval ranks and became chief of staff in 1928. Hitler named him commander in chief in 1935, and thereafter Raeder was responsible for the rapid expansion of the German navy. During the war, he was a vocal advocate of unrestricted U-boat warfare. Raeder, who received a 10-year sentence at the Nuremberg war crimes trials, died in 1960. Hitler and Raeder are seen together here at a naval review on the outbreak of war in Europe.

—Courtesy of Mrs. Robert Goralski

The first U.S. Navy ship hit by Japanese gunfire in 1941 was the river gunboat *Tutuila,* on July 30, more than four months before Pearl Harbor. A single bomb from one of 26 Japanese navy planes attacking Chunking, China, hit the vessel. Japan apologized the following day, saying the incident was an accident.

★★★★★

The first U.S. Navy ship to fire a shot in anger at a German ship was the destroyer USS *Niblack* on April 10, 1941. The incident occurred just after the *Niblack* had rescued survivors from a torpedoed Dutch merchantman south of Iceland. The American warship's sonar detected a submarine within firing range and took offensive action by dropping depth charges. According to the *Niblack*'s log, the captain was unable to determine what, if any, damage was done to the U-boat but believed it managed to leave the area.

★★★★★

The first U.S. ship sunk by German U-boats in 1941 was the freighter SS *Robin Moore* on May 21, 1941. She was torpedoed in the South Atlantic en route to South America. President Roosevelt, however, didn't publicly comment on the sinking until a month later, when on June 20 he termed the attack "the act of an international outlaw."

★★★★★

The U.S. had the largest navy in World War II, with 19,000 ships of all types by war's end. The combined total of ships for all other combatant nations (Allied and Axis) was just over 5,000. New Zealand, with four ships, was the smallest navy. The U.S. Navy had eight aircraft carriers when it entered the war on December 7, 1941. By the end of the war, less than four years later, it had added 113 more flattops. Japan managed to add 15 carriers to its fleet during the war but ended the war with only two.

The largest aircraft carrier of any navy became part of the Japanese fleet on November 11, 1944, when the 59,000-ton *Shinano* (with a 30-centimeter-thick deck over concrete) went on line. However, this ship recorded the briefest period of sea duty of any major ship in the war. The American submarine *Archerfish* torpedoed and sank her on November 29 in the Kumano Sea. This was the largest submarine kill of the war.

★★★★★

The only naval action against the Allies during the Normandy invasion on June 6, 1944, was from a trio of German E-boats from the 5th Flotilla under the command of Lieutenant Commander Heinrich Hoffmann. The three little boats broke through a haze off the beaches at Normandy and suddenly found themselves face to face with the greatest naval armada ever assembled (more than 5,000 ships). Hoffmann's sailors fired 18 torpedoes and quickly retreated. Their effort resulted in 30 casualties sustained in the sinking of a Norwegian destroyer, *Svenner.*

★★★★★

The first major warship to be sunk by aircraft bombing in the war was the 8,350-ton German cruiser *Königsberg,* which was sunk at dock in Bergen, Norway, on April 10, 1940, by two bombs from British Blackburn Skuas. She was also the only German ship to be sunk twice during the war. Salvaged and restored, she was sunk again on September 22, 1944. A similar fate befell the Italian cruiser *Gorizia,* also sunk twice during the war. She was scuttled and first sunk off La Spezia on September 8, 1943. Salvaged and restored, she was sunk by the Allies in June 1944.

★★★★★

The only British aircraft carrier to make it through the war was HMS *Furious.* She had originally been a cruiser before being converted.

The first British naval victory in the war was the hunt and offensive action against the Graf Spee *in December 1939. The pocket battleship was one of three such German vessels designed to get around the restrictions of the Versailles Treaty following World War I. Light and fast though heavily armored and heavily gunned, the* Graf Spee *sank nine cargo ships in the South Atlantic between the opening of hostilities on September 1 and its own demise on December 17. Four days earlier the* Graf Spee *had been located off the coast of Uruguay and engaged by a trio of British cruisers: Achilles, Ajax, and Exeter. The battle that followed lasted for 14 hours before the* Graf Spee *headed for Montevideo and sought refuge in the Plate River. When neutral Uruguay ordered Captain Hans Langsdorff to leave, he blew the ship up rather than have it fall into Allied hands. The captain and his crew were promptly interred. Three days later, draped in a German Imperial Navy flag rather than the Nazi swastika, the veteran of the famous World War I Battle of Jutland ended his own life with a gunshot to the head.*

—National Archives photo

The first ship lost from German mining of ship lanes along the east coast of the U.S. was the merchant ship SS *Robert C. Tutle* on June 15, 1942. Weeks earlier a pair of German U-boats loaded with mines intended for placement in New York harbor were sunk before they could complete their mission.

★★★★★

The last American ship to be sunk in peacetime was the merchantman SS *Sagadahoc,* which was torpedoed by a German U-boat in the South Atlantic on December 3, 1941, four days before Pearl Harbor.

★★★★★

The only German aircraft carrier was the *Graf Zeppelin.* Her keel was laid in 1938, and she was launched later that year. However, the Zeppelin was not finished before Germany surrendered. During her construction there were also serious differences between the Kriegsmarine and Luftwaffe about the aircraft she would carry.

★★★★★

The British lost only one Swordfish torpedo biplane while at the same time sinking five Italian ships during the Battle of Cape Matapan off the southern tip of Greece, March 28, 1941. The Italians lost more than 2,400 sailors aboard the cruisers *Pola, Zara,* and *Fiume* plus two destroyers.

★★★★★

The first Canadian woman to serve at sea during the war was Fern Blodgett, who earned the distinction in June 1941 when she became a radio operator on the Norwegian cargo ship *Mosdale.* The *Mosdale* holds the record for wartime crossings of the Atlantic, having made the dangerous passage 98 times.

Ironically the first ship sunk by indiscriminate mine warfare was the Japanese passenger ship *Terukuni Maru,* which hit a German-laid mine in the Thames estuary on November 21, 1939.

The first German magnetic mine discovered by the British in the Thames estuary was on November 23, 1939. It was defused by Lieutenant Commander J. G. D. Ouvry. In November and December of 1939, 59 Allied and neutral ships representing 203,513 tons were sunk by German magnetic mines. The German magnetic mines remained on the seafloor and were activated by the magnetic field generated by a ship passing overhead. They were a great improvement over moored contact mines, which could be located by minesweepers, their cables cut, and then the mines themselves destroyed by small-arms fire. Britain overcame the magnetic mines through the use of an electric cable around ships' hulls, thereby countering the magnetic field.

★★★★★

The first ship designated as an escort aircraft carrier (Baby Flattop) was the SS *Mormacmail,* a converted cargo ship. It entered U.S. Navy service as the USS *Long Island.*

★★★★★

The first Japanese submarine sunk by aircraft fire in the war was *I-70* on December 10, 1941, by planes from the USS *Enterprise* (CV-6).

★★★★★

The first naval defeat ever sustained by Japan came at the hands of the U.S. in the Battle of Midway.

★★★★★

The first U.S. ship captured after the war began in Europe was the merchant ship *City of Flint,* by the German pocket battleship *Deutschland.*

The USS Franklin (CV-13) became the most decorated ship in naval history as a result of one action, her participation in the October 1944 invasion of the Philippines. Members of her crew received a record 500 awards, decorations, and citations, including two Medals of Honor, 19 Navy Crosses, 115 Bronze Stars, and 234 Letters of Commendation. The Franklin is seen here four days after the engagement.

—U.S. Navy photo

The USS *Franklin* (CV-13) sustained the most devastating attack against any ship in U.S. history that didn't sink. Seriously damaged and considered lost during the invasion of the Philippines in 1944, *"Big Ben,"** as she was affectionately known to her crew, received two direct hits from a Japanese dive bomber. One 500-pound bomb penetrated to the hangar deck, igniting gasoline reservoirs, which in turn caused tremendous explosions of stored ammunition. Scores of fully fueled aircraft, their bomb racks loaded, were blown apart, killing everyone there. Violent explosions also consumed all aircraft waiting to take off on the flight deck. In all, over 800 of the *Franklin*'s crew were killed and nearly 400 others injured. When the ship was dead in the water and all but written off as lost by nearly everyone else, the commanding officer, Captain Leslie E. Gehres, responded to a question with the famous reply: "Abandon? Hell, we're still afloat!" Gehres was the first U.S. Navy enlisted man to rise through the ranks and eventually be named commander of an aircraft carrier. He received one of the 19 Navy Crosses crew members were awarded. Even when the still burning, stricken ship was finally taken in tow, Japanese planes repeatedly attacked her.

★★★★★

The USS *Laffey* (DD-724), nicknamed the Ship That Would Not Die, experienced the most extensive Japanese aircraft attack against any U.S. ship in the war when it was attacked by 22 planes, including several kamikaze, struck by two bombs, and heavily straffed while on radar picket duty 30 miles northwest of Okinawa on April 16, 1945. The *Laffey* shot down eight enemy planes and damaged six more before they crashed on board. The *Laffey* is the only surviving destroyer of the *USS Allen M. Sumner* class and is open for public viewing as part of the Patriot's Point Naval and Maritime Museum in Charlestown, S.C.

The worst naval defeat sustained by the Allies during the war was the February 27 to March 1, 1942, Battle of the Java Sea. The Japanese Imperial Navy sank 10 U.S., British, and Dutch ships during the engagement (plus four of its own!).

The Japanese ship that sank the most Japanese ships was the heavy cruiser *Mikuma*. Some sources credit her with sinking four Japanese transports on February 28, 1942, while attempting to hit the cruiser USS *Houston* during a follow-up engagement to the Battle of the Java Sea. (NOTE: *In his book* But Not in Shame, *John Toland cites Japanese sources as saying the four transports were accidentally sunk by torpedoes from the heavy cruisers* Mikuma *and* Mogami. *However, in* The Two-Ocean War, *naval historian Samuel Eliot Morison disputes this, claiming that the cruisers were too far away to score with torpedoes and that Panjang Island lay between them and the transports.*)

★★★★★

The largest fleet assembled in Japanese naval history was the one it moved against the U.S. in the Battle of Midway, June 4–6, 1942. The total fleet consisted of more than a hundred ships, including 11 battleships and eight aircraft carriers. By the time it was over the tide of the war in the Pacific had turned in favor of the U.S. Four of the Japanese carriers were sunk: *Akagi, Kaga, Soryu,* and *Hiryu,* all of which had participated in the Pearl Harbor attack. The 36,500-ton *Akagi,* which had been the flagship on December 7, became the first Japanese ship to be scuttled in the war. It was sunk by friendly fire after receiving serious damage at Midway. Japan also lost the heavy cruiser *Mikuma* and 332 aircraft. U.S. losses included the aircraft carrier USS *Yorktown* (CV-5) and the destroyer USS *Hammann.* The resounding American victory over a numerically superior enemy force a scant six months after the shock of Pearl Harbor was due to the U.S. Navy's ability to read Japanese codes and use the information to gain a tactical advantage.

*Contrary to popular belief the *Franklin,* despite the "Big Ben" nickname, was *not* named in honor of Benjamin Franklin but rather for the Civil War engagement the Battle of Franklin (Tennessee).

The first U.S. aircraft carrier sunk in the war was the USS Lexington (CV-2), on May 8, 1942, during the Battle of the Coral Sea. It was the first naval battle in which opposing ships never saw each other: all gunfire exchanged with ships was by planes from U.S. and Japanese aircraft carriers. In this photo crew members can be seen lowering themselves into the water shortly after the order to abandon ship was given. Survivors are being hauled aboard an unidentified U.S. Navy ship in the right photo.
—U.S. Navy photo

The first warship captured by the U.S. Navy was U-505, some 150 miles off Spanish Sahara, Africa (halfway between the Canaries and Cape Verdes), on June 4, 1944 by ships in the USS Guadalcanal (CVE-60) escort carrier group. In this photo Captain Daniel V. Gallery of the Guadalcanal is seen on the conning tower of U-505. At right, a whaleboat passes a towline from the Guadalcanal to U-505.

—U.S. Navy photos

★★★★★

The capture of the German U-boat 505 was the first time since 1814 that U.S. naval forces had boarded and taken an enemy ship. The submarine surfaced after being damaged by depth charges during an attack by U.S. antisubmarine surface ships, including the destroyer escorts *Chatelain* and *Pillsbury*. The U-boat's captain, believing reports from his crew that the submarine was sinking, surfaced. A party from the *Pillsbury* boarded and secured *U–505*. It was taken in tow by the *Guadalcanal* (which later passed the job onto a fleet tug) and is now on permanent display at the Museum of Science and Industry in Chicago, Ill.

★★★★★

The worst U.S. naval defeat ever in a fair fight was the 32-minute-long August 9, 1942, Battle of Savo Island. The U.S. Navy lost three heavy cruisers and one destroyer, 1,270 men killed, and 709 wounded. A fourth cruiser, the Australian HMAS *Canberra*, was also lost. Japan sustained negligible damage to their ships, lost 35 men, and reported another 57 wounded. The battle resulted in the greatest number of ships of the same class sunk in a single action when three heavy cruisers of the USS *New Orleans*–class were destroyed in ten minutes: USS *Vincennes*; USS *Quincy*; and USS *Astoria*.

The greatest naval battle of all time was the Battle for Leyte Gulf at the end of October 1944. It marked Japan's first use of kamikaze suicide planes. The U.S. force of 166 warships and 1,280 planes dominated Japan's 70 warships and 716 planes. Japan lost 34 ships, including four aircraft carriers and three battleships. The U.S. lost six ships. More than 56,260 Japanese died in the conflict; American deaths were 2,888. Vice Admiral Jisaburo Ozawa's fleet was sacrificed in an effort to lure away U.S. Admiral William F. Halsey's ships.

—U.S. Navy photo

The second aircraft carrier to carry the name USS Yorktown *(CV-10) was christened on April 15, 1943. Ten months later she celebrated the 7,000th landing on her decks. Her total landings in the war were 31,170. The* Yorktown *earned 15 battle stars and set several records for the fastest launches and recoveries of aircraft and the heaviest flying schedules. She also set a record for shooting down the most enemy aircraft, 14.5. Planes from her decks accounted for another 458 enemy aircraft shot down in the air and 695 on the ground. The* Yorktown *is now a public memorial at Patriots Point, Charleston, S.C.*
—*Patriot's Point photo*

The largest single loss of life involving a warship in history was the sinking of the 72,809-ton battleship *Yamato,* one of the two largest battleships in the world. Only 269 personnel from the 3,292 member crew survived. *Yamato* was sunk after three hours of bombing and torpedo attacks by aircraft from U.S. Task Force 58 during the Okinawa campaign in April 1945. Those lost included Admiral Seiichi Ito, the last Japanese admiral to command a major naval force in battle against the U.S. Navy. Ito was killed on April 8, 1945, while leading the 10-ship action in the East China Sea. Six of the Japanese ships were lost in the battle. Of the 900 U.S. aircraft involved, only 10 were lost.

★★★★★

The largest single loss of U.S. Navy personnel at sea, 883 lives, was in the sinking of the cruiser USS *Indianapolis* on July 30, 1945. The *Indianapolis* was operating under secret orders while participating in Operation Bronx Shipments, the delivery of matériel and components for the atom bomb to Tinian Island on July 26, when she was hit by a pattern of six torpedoes fired by Japanese submarine *I–58.* The cruiser sank in 12 minutes. Because of the fact that the *Indianapolis* had been operating under secret orders with her route, destination, and mission classified, it took longer than would be expected for her to be noticed as missing and more than 96 hours before the 316 survivors were picked out of the sea. Ironically, more members of the *Indianapolis* crew died from shark attacks than had been killed in the torpedoing and sinking.

★★★★★

The only underwater collision between two U.S. submarines was on February 25, 1945, when the USS *Hoe* and USS *Flounder* apparently needed more room to navigate than they had off Indochina. Neither sub sank.

Germany's second most successful U-boat captain, Wolfgang Luth, was accidentally shot and killed by a sentry when he failed to properly identify himself near the headquarters of Admiral Karl Doenitz. Luth commanded four different U-boats in the war, made 14 patrols, and sank 44 enemy ships, just one short of Otto Kretschmer's record.

★★★★★

USS *Torsk* is credited with being the last U.S. submarine to fire a torpedo and sink a combatant enemy ship on August 14, 1945, the day before the Pacific war ended. The *Torsk,* which was commissioned in December 1944, is now a public submarine memorial exhibit open to the public in Baltimore, Md.

★★★★★

The only chaplain in the war to receive a Congressional Medal of Honor was Joseph O'Callahan, USN, who earned the distinction for heroism aboard the aircraft carrier USS *Franklin* (CV-13) during the invasion of the Philippines in 1944.

★★★★★

The greatest aircraft carrier engagement of the war was the Battle of the Philippines Sea. The Allies had 15 carriers against nine for the Japanese. Overall fleet sizes were Allies, 112 ships; Japan, 55 ships.

★★★★★

The last major warship sunk in World War II was the cruiser USS *Indianapolis* on July 30, 1945.

★★★★★

The only U.S. Navy officer court-martialed for losing a ship in the war was Captain Charles McVay, commanding officer of the USS *Indianapolis.*

Because the USS Intrepid *(CV-11) was the most frequently hit U.S. ship in the war, she earned the dubious nickname* The Evil I *in some quarters. To most who sailed on her, however, she was affectionately known as* The Fighting I. *In the two photos* Intrepid *is seen as she appeared in the war and as she looks today. Aircraft from the Intrepid's decks sank the two largest battleships ever built: the* Yamato *and* Musashi *which both weighed 72,809 tons. During 15 months of combat the Intrepid's guns and planes sank a total of 80 Japanese ships and 650 aircraft.*

In the post–World War II period the Intrepid *served as the primary recovery ship during two Project Mercury and Project Gemini space missions. Known today as the Intrepid Sea-Air-Space Museum, it is permanently docked at Pier 86 on West 46th Street in New York City.*
—U.S. Navy photo
—Intrepid Sea-Air-Space Museum photo

The first naval battle in which opposing ships never saw each other was the Battle of the Coral Sea, May 3–8, 1942. (The battle actually took place in its northern bight, the Solomon Sea.) The battle was an exchange between carrier aircraft against opposing ships. The Japanese sank the carrier USS *Lexington* (CV-2), the destroyer USS *Sims*, and the fleet oiler USS *Neosho* and damaged the carrier USS *Yorktown* (CV-5). U.S. naval flyers sank the destroyer *Kikuzuki* and three other ships plus the aircraft carrier *Shoho*, which holds the record time of any Japanese ship in the war for going to the bottom: 10 minutes. Each side lost about 30 planes. Although Japan lost five ships versus three for the U.S., the Americans' ships represented the greater tonnage loss. The Battle of the Coral Sea is generally regarded as Japan's first naval defeat of the war because their intention to invade Australia was thwarted. (NOTE: *The Lexington was not actually sunk by the Japanese but so badly damaged that the American destroyer USS* Phelps *administered the coup de grace afterward.*)

★★★★★

The first order authorizing the German navy to seek and destroy Soviet submarines, under the cloak of claiming to mistake them for British ships, was issued on June 15, 1941. The German directive called for the "annihilation of Russian submarines without any trace, including their crews." It specifically mentioned submarines found south of the Aland Islands. This was a week before Germany invaded Russia and at a time when the two countries were still at peace.

★★★★★

The first Battle of Narvik (Norway) on April 10, 1940, resulted in Britain and Germany each losing two destroyers. However, after the engagement broke off, five German ships that had participated in the sea battle were tracked and eventually destroyed by the British.

The USS *Enterprise* (CV-6) earned more battle stars (20) in World War II than any warship in U.S. history. Aircraft from the *Big E* sank 71 enemy ships and destroyed 911 enemy aircraft. Despite her record, the *Enterprise* was sold for scrap after the war. On January 18, 1946, she made port along the South Wall of the U.S. Naval Base in Bayonne, N.J., and never went to sea as a fighting ship again. *Enterprise* was decommissioned at 1:47 P.M., February 17, 1947, and became a member of the Atlantic Reserve Fleet. Each Memorial Day for the next decade the *Big E* was the most visited of the several World War II warships in reserve at Bayonne. In 1957 the Navy announced plans to sell the *Enterprise* for scrap. Admiral William F. Halsey used his influence to delay the order while efforts were made to raise private funds to preserve her. But this was not to be. In the summer of 1958 the *Enterprise*, with the assistance of tugboats, left the navy base, passed under Bayonne Bridge, and slowly moved up Newark Bay and the Hackensack River. She made her final port at the old Federal Shipyard site in Kearney, N.J. In early 1959 men with torches and pneumatic hammers did what the Japanese Imperial Navy had not been able to do, and the *Enterprise* ceased to exist.

★★★★★

The largest amphibious operation in the war was Operation Husky, the invasion of Sicily on July 10, 1943, in which 1,375 ships were directly involved plus an additional 36 ships used in support covering operations. The planning was made particularly difficult because it was not until the middle of May (when the North Africa campaign ended) that Allied planners knew exactly how many divisions they would have. During the initial assault seven divisions, one armored combat team, two commando brigades, and an assault brigade were to be put ashore against an enemy who was, at least on paper, almost equal in numbers. The D-Day invasion of Normandy exceeds it only if follow-up amphibious landings are counted.

The first kamikaze attacks ever took place during the Battle for Leyte Gulf on October 25, 1944. The first ship sunk as a result of a kamikaze attack was the 6,730-ton escort carrier USS St.-Lô (CVE-63) a few minutes before 11 A.M. The photo shows a second kamikaze destroyed in midair before impact on the St.-Lô. The first U.S. ship crashed by a kamikaze had been the escort carrier USS Santee at 7:40 A.M. The last U.S. ship sunk by a kamikaze was the destroyer USS Callaghan, off Okinawa on July 28, 1945. By war's end kamikazes would sink or damage more than 300 ships, causing more than 15,000 U.S. casualties.

—U.S. Navy photo

The only submarine credited with sinking a fleet aircraft carrier was Japan's *I-19*, which sank the USS *Hasp* (CV-7) near Espíritu Santo on September 15, 1942. The American carrier had to be finished off by friendly fire from destroyers. The commander of *I-19* was Takaichi Kinashi, Japan's leading submarine officer. The U.S. also lost two escort carriers to submarines: USS *Liscome Bay*, off Tarawa, November 24, 1943, and USS *Block Island* on May 29, 1944, off the Madeira Islands.

★★★★★

The first U.S. ship sunk in U.S. coastal waters was the USS *Jacob Jones*, a destroyer, which was torpedoed by German U-boat *578* off New Jersey on February 28, 1942.

★★★★★

The first submarine sunk as a result of Hedgehog fire (cluster bombs) was *I-175* on February 5, 1944. Hedgehogs and a smaller version called Mouse-traps were adopted by the U.S. Navy in 1942. They consisted of clusters of bombs that broke into a pattern after being fired from a surface ship.

★★★★★

The first U.S. submarine to sink a Japanese submarine was the USS *Gudgeon*, under the command of Lieutenant Commander Joseph Grenfell, which, on January 27, 1942, sank *I-173*.

★★★★★

USS *Batfish* is the only submarine to sink three enemy submarines in three days. In February 1945, on her sixth war patrol, the *Batfish* encountered and sank three of the four known Japanese submarines around the Philippines. *Batfish* is now a memorial exhibit in Muskogee, Okla.

The first action against foreign ships in U.S. ports was on May 15, 1941, when armed U.S. troops boarded and took into protective custody the luxury liner *Normandie* and 10 other French ships. The U.S. renamed her the SS *Lafayette*. However, it burned at dockside in New York in February 1942 and had to be scrapped.

★★★★★

The only known instance in which a U.S. submarine sank itself involved the USS *Tullibee* on March 26, 1944. The *Tullibee*, in the waters off Palau in the Carolines, fired two torpedoes at a Japanese transport. One of the torpedoes turned and made a complete circle, hitting and sinking the *Tullibee*.

★★★★★

The only known instance in which a submarine sank because a crew member failed to secure one of its torpedo doors was Japan's loss of *I-169* off the island of Truk. The sub was forced to make an emergency dive to escape attacking U.S. aircraft.

★★★★★

The first submarine sunk by aircraft fire was Italy's *Argonauta*, by an RAF Sunderland on June 28, 1940.

★★★★★

The only U.S. submarine credited with sinking a battleship was the USS *Sealion II*, which torpedoed Japan's 36,610-ton *Kongo* off Foochow, China, on November 21, 1944.

★★★★★

The 785 submarines Germany lost in the war was greater than the collective total of all other major combatant nations: Japan lost 129; Italy, 107; Britain, 74; the U.S., 52; the Soviet Union, 50.

The first U.S. Navy PT boat (#9) arrived in New York from Great Britain two days after World War II had begun in September 1939. It had been purchased there by Henry R. Sutphen, executive vice president of the Electric Boat Company, which had its Elco Naval Division in Bayonne, N.J. Sutphen used his British-purchased boat as a model for the hundreds of others made at the Bayonne facility. The Navy took delivery of this original boat from Elco in June 1940 and designated it PT-9. By the time Pearl Harbor was attacked, several manufacturers were offering designs of what were called the Plywood Derbys of 1941. The most famous of all Elco boats was John F. Kennedy's PT-109.

—Bayonne Times *photo by Henry Manger*
—*Author's collection*

Pound for pound, the most heavily armed vessels in the U.S. Navy were the deadly and highly maneuverable PT boats.

★★★★★

The only U.S. ship sunk by Japanese *Kaitens* (one-man suicide torpedos) was the merchantman SS *Mississinewa* in October 1944.

★★★★★

The first Japanese surface ship sunk by aerial attack in the war was the destroyer *Kisaragi*, by U.S. Marine aircraft defending Wake Island on December 11, 1941.

★★★★★

The first Japanese attack on a military base on the U.S. mainland occurred at Fort Stevens, Oreg., on June 22, 1942, when a Japanese submarine fired at the coastal outpost. There were no casualties. The last time a mainland military outpost had been fired on by a foreign power was during the War of 1812. The first Japanese attack against Canada was in June 1942, when a submarine fired on a radio station on Vancouver Island.

    The first U.S. civilian facility on the mainland to come under enemy fire in the war was the oil fields west of Santa Barbara, Calif. They were fired on by Japanese submarine *I-17* on February 23, 1942.

★★★★★

The first city to come under naval bombardment in the war was Danzig, by the German battleship *Schleswig-Holstein* on September 1, 1939.

★★★★★

Italy lost eight hospital ships during the war, the greatest number of any combatant nation.

The only U.S. submarine skipper relieved of command of a Japanese submarine was Hiram Cassedy. Cassedy had been assigned to accept the surrender at sea of one of three Japanese I-class submarines designed and built to torpedo the Panama Canal. Cassedy violated strict orders not to take souvenirs when he passed out swords to his officers. Admiral William F. Halsey removed him from command of his boat and the Japanese sub.

★★★★★

The first British naval victory over an Axis power was in mid-March 1941, against the Italians in the Mediterranean.

★★★★★

The first U.S. submarine to sink a Japanese destroyer was S-44, which sank the *Kako* on August 10, 1942.

★★★★★

The first U.S. Navy escort protection for British ships leaving U.S. and Canadian ports began on September 17, 1941.

★★★★★

The first U.S. Navy ship named in honor of a black American was the destroyer USS *Harmon*, on July 25, 1943.

    The first black American commissioned in the U.S. Navy was Ensign Bernard Robinson in June 1942.

★★★★★

The first Japanese submarine sunk by aircraft fire in the war was *I-70*, on December 10, 1941, by planes from the USS *Enterprise* (CV-6).

The last U.S. aircraft carrier sunk in the war was the USS Princeton (CVL-23), on October 24, 1944, during the Battle of the Sibuyan Sea (the first of the four major engagements that constitute the Battle for Leyte Gulf). In the top photo the Princeton *is unidentifiable in the tremendous geyser of smoke and flame after a direct hit by Japanese land-based aircraft. The bomb passed through several decks of the light carrier and exploded among stowed torpedoes.* Princeton *survivors are about to be picked up by the USS* Cosin Young *(DD-743).*

—*U.S. Navy photo*

The first battleship to launch an aircraft from her decks was the USS Texas (BB-35), commissioned in 1914 and a veteran of both world wars. Its first catapulting of a plane actually took place pre–World War II. In 1948 the Texas became the first battleship established as a state shrine. She is open to public view at San Jacinto State Park, Tex.

—U.S. Navy photo

122

The youngest person to serve aboard a U.S. Navy ship in combat was 12-year-old Calvin Graham, who won a Bronze Star and Purple Heart on USS *South Dakota* (BB-57) before the Navy found out he had incorrectly reported his age when he enlisted.

★★★★★

The battleship most often reported sunk by the Japanese was USS *North Carolina* (BB-55), which was said to have been destroyed six times during her 40 months at sea. Runner-up was USS *South Dakota* (BB-57), said to have gone to the deep five times.

★★★★★

The only state in the U.S. that has never had a battleship named after it is Montana. Work was started on a battleship that was to be named *Montana* during World War I, and in World War II a Montana-class was also begun, but in both cases the wars ended before the ships were finished.

★★★★★

The only Japanese battleship still floating at the time of the surrender was the 42,785-ton *Nagato*. In terms of size, the 725-foot-long warship was the 19th-largest battleship in the war. (NOTE: *See the appendix for a listing of the 20 largest battleships.*)

★★★★★

The first successful attack by aircraft against ships was the November 11, 1940, raid by 20 British Swordfish torpedo biplanes from the aircraft carrier *Illustrious* against the Italian naval base at Taranto. The British planes came in at under 40 feet above sea level. The Royal Navy lost two planes versus severe damage to nearly half of the Italian battle fleet. A trio of capital ships, *Conte di Cavour, Littorio,* and *Duilio,* remained out of action for much of the war.

The first Liberty ship built by the U.S. was the SS *Patrick Henry* in September 1941. The last Liberty ship was the SS *Benjamin Warner* in 1944. In all, more than 2,740 went to sea. The only Liberty ship still in existence is the SS *Jeremiah O'Brian,* built in May 1943. It is now a memorial open to the public in San Francisco.

The first Liberty ship to be launched just 10 days after the keel was laid was the SS *Joseph N. Teal* in October 1942.

The first black to take command of a Liberty ship was Captain Hugh Mulzac, skipper of the SS *Booker T. Washington.*

★★★★★

The first major U.S. naval engagement in the Pacific was the Battle of Makassar Strait on January 24, 1942. Four American destroyers intercepted and engaged a Japanese invasion force headed for the petroleum farms at Balikpapan, Borneo. The outnumbered U.S. destroyers sank four Japanese troop transports, inflicting heavy casualties.

★★★★★

The first U.S. naval-air offensive in the Pacific was the February 1, 1942, attack against Japanese air and naval bases in the Marshall and Gilbert islands. The U.S. force consisted of two aircraft carriers, five cruisers, and 10 destroyers.

★★★★★

The largest naval armada assembled in the war was for the Normandy invasion. American records say 5,000 ships were involved, whereas the British state a more conservative 4,500.

The first wave of troops to hit the beaches at Normandy on D-Day was brought ashore by ships from Task Force O, Rear Admiral John L. Hall commanding. They landed at Omaha Beach.

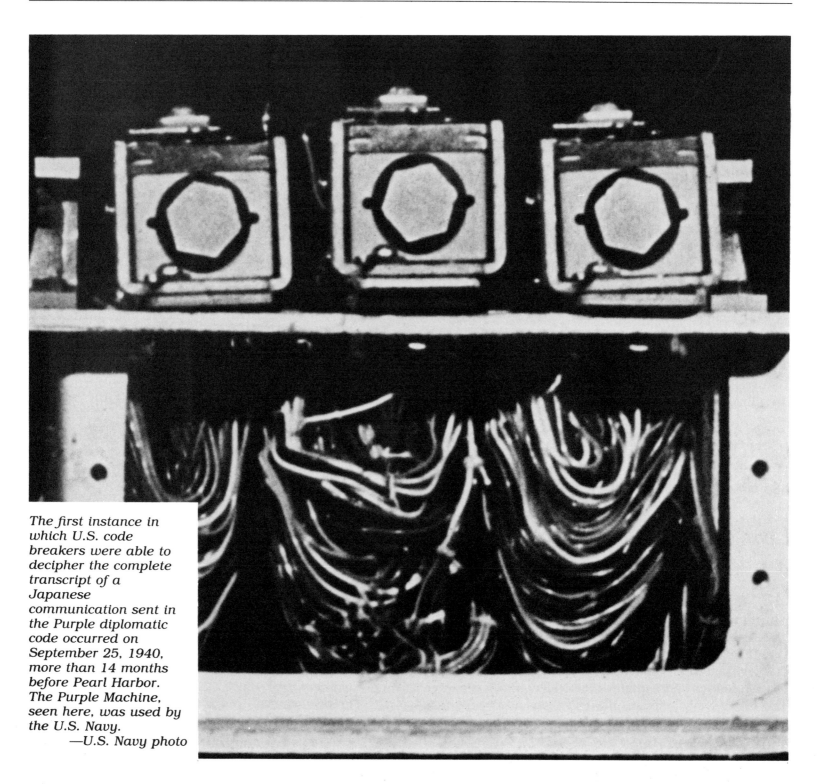

The first instance in which U.S. code breakers were able to decipher the complete transcript of a Japanese communication sent in the Purple diplomatic code occurred on September 25, 1940, more than 14 months before Pearl Harbor. The Purple Machine, seen here, was used by the U.S. Navy.
　　　　—U.S. Navy photo

The two most significant intelligence breakthroughs in the war were the ability of the U.S. to read Japanese Purple code traffic and Britain's reading of Germany's Enigma code traffic. Credit for the Purple intelligence is generally given to U.S. Army Colonel William Friedman, who spent three years attempting what many critics considered a two-pronged impossible task: (a) to determine the operating principles of and then replicate the mechanical encoding and decoding devices the Japanese were using without ever having seen one, and (b) once that was done, to discover the correct cryptographic sequences used. However, it was the genius of a civilian cryptanalyst, Harry Larry Clark, who triggered the actual breakthrough.

The first capture of an Enigma coding machine took place on May 7, 1941, when British sailors from HMS *Somali* boarded and captured the 139-foot-long steam-powered German weather ship *München* in the North Atlantic. Armed with a single machine gun, the crew of the small German ship abandoned the vessel after a number of near hits fired by the *Somali*. Because a number of the *München*'s sea cocks had been rendered inaccessible when her sea ballast was replaced by concrete (to strengthen her against icebergs), no effort was made to scuttle the ship.

The first German U-boat captured by the Allies was *U-110* on May 9, 1941, by the Royal Navy's HMS *Bulldog* and HMS *Broadway* in the North Atlantic. More significantly, however, was the fact that the British had obtained their second Enigma coding machine in 72 hours. But the submarine sank while in tow the following day.

★★★★★

The aircraft carrier HMS *Hermes* was the last British warship sunk in the Pacific war. The *Hermes* was lost off Ceylon on April 9, 1942, as a result of Japanese aircraft fire. This is not to be confused with the British destroyer also named *Hermes*, which was given to the Greeks, then captured and put into service by the Germans.

The last surface-to-surface engagement of the war was on March 30, 1945 at Okinawa when the USS Irwin (DD-794) sank two Japanese torpedo/patrol crafts.

★★★★★

"The Fightingest Ship in the Royal Canadian Navy" was the destroyer HMCS *Haida*, which saw action in the English Channel and Bay of Biscay. She is credited with destroying 14 enemy ships. The *Haida* is now a memorial open to the public at Ontario.

★★★★★

The only U.S. Navy admiral to have the unfortunate distinction of having two aircraft carriers lost while he was aboard them is Admiral Frank J. Fletcher. He was on the USS *Yorktown* (CV-5) at Midway and the USS *Lexington* (CV-2) in the Battle of the Coral Sea. Fletcher, who had been awarded the Medal of Honor in 1914 for action in the Vera Cruz campaign, was also on the USS *Saratoga* (CV-3) when she was hit by, and survived, a Japanese torpedo attack.

★★★★★

The first two U.S. aircraft carriers to be converted from battle cruiser hulls were the USS *Lexington* (CV-2) and USS *Saratoga* (CV-3). The conversions were provided for in the Washington Naval Disarmament treaty after World War I. The U.S. was permitted to convert two existing hulls into aircraft carriers of 33,000 tons each. In reality both topped out at just over 36,000 tons when "legal" modifications were added.

★★★★★

The Navy's first aircraft carrier, USS *Langley* (CV-1), had been converted from the 5,500-ton fleet collier USS *Jupiter* (AC.3). The *Jupiter*, and a sister ship that had been lost in an accident in 1918, were coal-carrying supply ships that became obsolete with the introduction of oil as an energy source for the fleet.

The last commander in chief of the Kriegsmarine (German navy) in the war was Admiral Hans Georg von Freideburg (left). He is seen here with Colonel General P. F. Stumpf, the last commander of the Luftwaffe (center), and Field Marshall Wilhelm Keitel, the last commander in chief of the army (right), on May 7, 1945, after signing surrender documents at Soviet army headquarters in Berlin. Von Freideburg committed suicide shortly afterward.

—U.S. Army photo

126

The first U-boat sunk by the U.S. was *U-656*, which was torpedoed from the air of Cape Race, Newfoundland, by Ensign William Tepuni while piloting a Navy Lockheed-Hudson on March 1, 1942.

★★★★★

The first U-boat sunk by a U.S. Navy surface ship was *U-85*, on April 15, 1942, off Wemble Shoal near Hatteras, by Lieutenant Commander H. W. Howe of the destroyer USS *Roper*.

★★★★★

The first U.S. submarine sunk in the war was the *Sealion*, at Cavite Naval Station in the Philippines on December 19, 1941. The *Sealion* had been in port for overhauling and was badly damaged during the December 10 raid by Japanese aircraft. She was sunk by three U.S. Navy depth charges after being stripped of still useful equipment. The last U.S. submarine sunk in the war was the *Bullhead*, on August 6, 1945, the day the atom bomb was dropped on Hiroshima.

★★★★★

The first U.S. submarine sunk in the Atlantic was *S-26*, off Panama on January 24, 1942. The last U.S. submarine sunk in the Atlantic was the *Dorado*, on October 12, 1943.

★★★★★

The branch of the U.S. military that sustained the highest casualty rate was the submarine service, with 22 percent. For every U.S. surface-ship sailor lost in the war, six U.S. submarines lost their lives. One out of every seven submariners died: 3,505 officers and enlisted men. It was the heaviest ratio of any branch of the U.S. armed services, including the Marines. One out of every five submarines was lost. In the Pacific 49 were sunk, and three were lost in the Atlantic.

The only U.S. submarine to be sunk by a Japanese submarine was the USS *Corvina*, which was sunk off Truk on November 16, 1943, by *I-176*.

★★★★★

The last submarine to sink another submarine was the USS *Spikefish*, which sank *I-373* on August 13, 1945, one day before Japan agreed to the surrender.

★★★★★

The first U.S. ship sunk by a Japanese submarine was SS *Cynthia Olson*, by *I-26*, approximately 750 miles from the U.S. mainland's west coast on December 7, 1941. This submarine was also responsible for the greatest loss of life involving members of one family when the five Sullivan brothers died during the sinking of the USS *Juneau* in the naval battle of Guadalcanal, November 12–15, 1942.

★★★★★

The first Allied warship sunk by a submarine was British fleet carrier HMS *Courageous* on September 17, 1939, by *U-29* under the command of Otto Schuart. According to Royal Navy records, 519 members of the 22,500-ton ship's crew perished when it went to the bottom of the sea in the Western Approaches off southwestern Ireland. The aircraft carrier was on antisubmarine duty at the time. After the sinking the Royal Navy removed fleet carriers from this duty.

★★★★★

The first German U-boat sunk was *U-39*, by British destroyers in the Atlantic, on September 14, 1939. At the outbreak of war Germany had 45 battle-ready U-boats out of a fleet of 57. Nine others were under construction. By February 1943, during the Battle of the Atlantic, Germany had 409 U-boats in active service. They reached their peak in May 1943 when there were 425 at large.

One of the best-kept secrets prior to the Normandy invasion was the creation of man-made harbors, code-named Mulberries, which consisted of 145 very large concrete caissons that the Allies towed across the English Channel and sank in tandem to create a breakwater near the assault beaches. The largest caisson resembled a five-story building on its side. Pontoon piers permitted trucks to reach them and receive matériel being brought in. Mulberry ruins are still visible at Normandy, and during low tide can be reached on foot.
—Photo by author

The first U.S. naval action of significance against territory Japan regarded as part of her home land was the June, 1944 bombardment and invasion of Saipan. Japanese Zero is seen here moments before it misses unidentified U.S. aircraft carrier at start of campaign on June 15.

—U.S. Navy photo

The USS Massachusetts (BB-59) fired the first and last 16-inch guns in the war. The debut was in November 1942 during Operation Torch, the invasion of North Africa, and the last was in 1945 at Honshu, Japan. The Massachusetts is now open to the public as part of the warships exhibit at Battleship Cove in Fall River, Mass.

—U.S. Navy photo

The USS Missouri (BB-63) was the last of the Iowa-class battleships to be completed. Commissioned on 11 June 1944, she was destined to become one of the most famous warships in the U.S. Navy. It wasn't her war record but rather the Japanese surrender on her decks that gained her fame.

—U.S. Navy photo

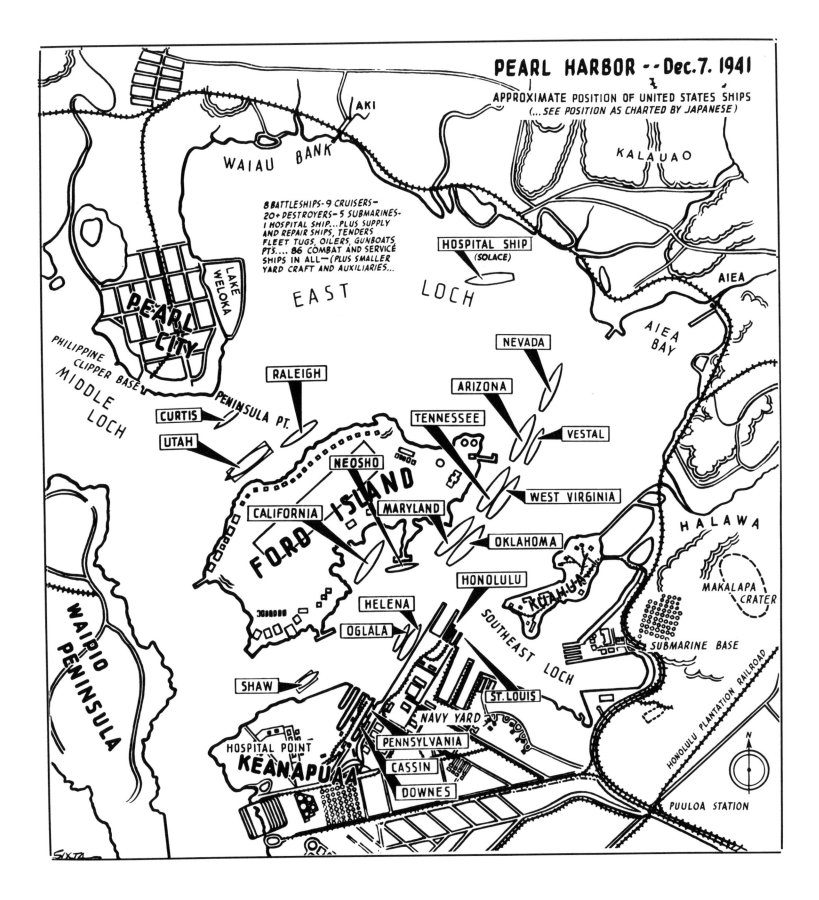

SPECIAL SECTION

December 7, 1941

"A Day That Will Live in Infamy"

Because the Japanese surprise attack on Pearl Harbor and other U.S. military installations in Hawaii was the impetus that thrust the U.S. into the war, numerous events obviously happened for the first time on what President Franklin D. Roosevelt would call "a day that will live in infamy."

However, did the Japanese attack really come as a total surprise? Were there no indications that relations with Japan were seriously strained?

Perhaps the attack in the Pacific seemed to come from out of the blue to many a man on the street. The real and present danger, after all, was the Austrian paperhanger with the funny little mustache. By December 7, 1941, Hitler and his Axis cohorts had most of the European continent captive or trembling in fear, and his crack fighting units were already deep into the Soviet Union. Only Britain seemed to be standing between him and the total conquest of Europe.

But the threat of war with Japan was indeed well known in high echelons of the U.S. government and military. In fact, an extraordinary number of signs indicated that war was not only possible, it was inevitable.

Over the past five decades historians have pointed to numerous incidents they felt should have alerted the U.S. that war with Japan was imminent. Many have asked out loud how this country could have been caught so seemingly unprepared. Revisionists have long proffered the charge that President Roosevelt and other high officials in the American government knew the Japanese were going to attack Pearl Harbor but let it happen as a means of getting America into the war.

The pros and cons of this debate were brought to the fore and explored in depth during the 1980s in four magnificent books about Pearl Harbor: Gordon Prange's *At Dawn He Slept*, John Toland's *Infamy*, and Prange's two follow-ups, *Dec. 7, 1941*, and *Pearl Harbor: The Verdict of History* (both published after Prange's death with contributions by coauthors Donald M. Goldstein and Katherine V. Dillon).

Toland's book suggests Roosevelt and others knew. In *Pearl Harbor*, Prange and his coauthors strongly contend he did not. Nonetheless, the litany of unheeded warnings, opportunities missed, and ironies connected to the Pearl Harbor attack are astonishing.

In this special section to mark the 50th anniversary of America's entry into the war, we have gathered some of the more interesting items about it and present them in concise form along with Pearl Harbor superlatives.

Japanese Special Envoy Saburo Kurusu and Ambassador Kichisaburo wait outside Secretary of State Cordell Hull's office to present their country's demands early Sunday morning, December 7, 1941. The meeting took place at approximately the time the Japanese surprise attack on Pearl Harbor began. Because of the Purple intercept Hull already knew the agenda for their visit.

—National Archives photo

Time Was Running Out

Prior to hostilities in 1941 the U.S. had only eight Purple decoding machines, even though U.S. Army Colonel William Friedman had broken the code and designed the first machine on September 25, 1940, more than 14 months before Pearl Harbor. Of the eight machines in existence, one was originally slated for use by Admiral Husband E. Kimmel or General Walter C. Short in Hawaii. Four were based in Washington, with the Navy and Army having two each. One was sent to General MacArthur in the Philippines and two others were sent to London in exchange for the Ultra intelligence the British were getting from the German Enigma machines. When both Washington and London expressed strong interest in acquiring an additional machine, Hawaii was bypassed and it was sent to the British. In the absence of having a decoding machine in Hawaii, an amazing sequence of events followed:

- Would Admiral Kimmel or General Short have had the same reaction President Roosevelt did on December 6 after he read the 13-part message Tokyo sent to its ambassadors in Washington? "This means war," the President commented midway through his reading.
- The 14th part of the message, not decoded by Washington until the morning of December 7, set "1 P.M. Eastern Standard Time today" (7:30 A.M. in Honolulu) as the precise time Tokyo wanted its ambassadors to deliver the ultimatum.
- Instead of alerting Pearl Harbor through military communication channels, Washington sent Kimmel and Short a Western Union Telegram (in code) advising them of the 7:30 A.M. local time ultimatum.
- It reached the Western Union office in Honolulu 22 minutes before the attack, but for obvious reasons wasn't delivered until four hours later.
- It took another three hours before the message was decoded by intelligence officers in Pearl Harbor.

January 1941: "My Peruvian colleague told a member of my staff that he heard . . . that Japanese military forces planned . . . to attempt a surprise attack on Pearl Harbor." Considered one of the most remarkable dispatches ever sent by a U.S. diplomat, U.S. ambassador to Japan Joseph C. Grew sent the above to the State Department *within a month after Admiral Yamamoto first disclosed to anyone* his bold plan for attacking Pearl Harbor. However, it received only token interest in official circles.

★★★★★

January 24, 1941: "The security of the U.S. Pacific Fleet while in Pearl Harbor, and of the Pearl Harbor Naval Base itself, has been under renewed study by the Navy Department and forces afloat for the past several weeks. This reexamination has been, in part, prompted by the increased gravity of the situation with respect to Japan, and by reports from abroad of successful bombing and torpedo plane attacks on ships while in bases. If war eventuates with Japan, it is believed easily possible that hostilities would be initiated by a surprise attack upon the fleet or the naval base at Pearl Harbor." So said Secretary of the Navy Frank Knox in a letter to Secretary of War Henry L. Stimson some 11 months before the attack. The letter, which was actually written by Rear Admiral Richmond Kelly Turner and approved by Admiral Harold R. (Betty) Stark before Knox signed it, continued: "In my opinion the inherent possibilities of a major disaster to the fleet or naval base warrant taking every step, as rapidly as can be done, that will increase the joint readiness of the Army and Navy to withstand a raid of the character mentioned above."

★★★★★

February 1941: "It must be remembered too that a single submarine attack may indicate the presence of a considerable surface force . . . accompanied by a carrier." Remarks from Admiral Kimmel to Rear Admi-

The battleship USS Oklahoma (BB-37) was the first U.S. ship in Pearl Harbor to be hit by a Japanese torpedo. It was dropped by pilot Inichi Goto. The 29,000-ton Oklahoma, sister ship to the USS Nevada (BB-36) joined the fleet in 1915.

—U.S. Navy photo

ral Claude C. Bloch, the man he appointed as naval base defense commander for Pearl Harbor.

★★★★★

February 11, 1941: Ten months before Japan's surprise attack, Admiral Kimmel, Commander In Chief of the U.S. Fleet in Hawaii, issued a letter to his command that said in part: "A declaration of war might be preceded by . . . a surprise attack on ships in Pearl Harbor . . . a surprise submarine attack on ships in operating area . . . [or] a combination of these two."

★★★★★

February 18, 1941: "I feel that a surprise attack (submarine, air or combined) on Pearl Harbor is a possibility." Letter from Admiral Kimmel to Admiral Stark.

★★★★★

February 25, 1941: "In view of the Japanese situation, the Navy is concerned with the security of the fleet in Hawaii. . . . They are in the situation where they must guard against a surprise or trick attack. . . . We also have information regarding the possible use of torpedo planes. There is the possible introduction of Japanese carrier-based planes." Excerpted from remarks made by General George C. Marshall, U.S. Army Chief of Staff, to other officers. Eight days later Marshall urged General Short to send him a review of the Hawaii defenses against possible air attack, calling it "a matter of first priority."

★★★★★

March 1941: Rear Admiral Patrick N. L. Bellinger and Major General Frederick L. Martin authored the now famous, and prophetic, Martin-Bellinger Report for defending U.S. military installations in the Hawaiian Islands. Both officers were based in Oahu. Among the highlights of the report are observations such as

- "A successful, sudden raid against our ships and naval installations on Oahu might prevent effective offensive action by our forces in the Western Pacific for a long period. (NOTE: *Prior to hostilities, Orange was the identifying code name the U.S. military used when making reference to Japan in oral and written communications and in tactical planning.*)

- It appears Orange submarines and/or an Orange fast raiding force might arrive in Hawaiian waters with no prior warning from our intelligence service.

- Orange might send into this area one or more submarines and/or one or more fast raiding forces composed of carriers supported by fast cruisers.

- A declaration of war might be preceded by a surprise submarine attack on ships in the operating area or a surprise attack on Oahu, including ships and installations in Pearl Harbor.

- It appears that the most likely and dangerous form of attack on Oahu would be an air attack. Such an attack would most likely be launched from one or more carriers, which would probably approach inside 300 miles.

- Any single submarine attack might indicate the presence of a considerable undiscovered surface force.

- In a dawn air attack there is a high probability that it could be delivered as a complete surprise."

★★★★★

April 1, 1941: The following alert was sent to all Pacific commands by U.S. Naval Intelligence in Washington: "Personnel of your Naval Intelligence Service should be advised that because of the fact that past experience shows the Axis Powers often begin activities in a particular field on Saturdays and Sundays or on national holidays of the country concerned, they should take steps on such days to see that proper watches and precautions are in effect."

In a rare instance Hawaiian radio station KGMB, which did not normally broadcast overnight, was on the air the night and early morning hours of December 6–7. The station stayed on the air so an expected flight of U.S. B-17s from the mainland could use its signal as a guide. After the attack Japanese pilots admitted the station's signal had also helped their navigation to Pearl Harbor. Meanwhile, this B-17 was on the ground at Hickham Field when it was attacked.

—U.S. Navy photo

April 23, 1941: During a conversation in which Secretary of War Stimson speculated about the safety of U.S. forces in Hawaii in the event of hostilities with Japan, Army Chief of Staff General Marshall replied, "The Japs wouldn't dare attack Hawaii."

★★★★★

May 12, 1941: Some seven months before the attack, the U.S. Army and Navy held what the military described as "the greatest war drills ever staged" in the Hawaiian Islands. Army bombers "attacked" enemy aircraft carriers several hundred miles at sea just as one carrier was preparing to launch planes against the islands. In an ironic note, a formation of 21 B-17s landed on Oahu from the mainland while the "attack" was under way. The war games consisted of many phases and options and continued for two weeks, with the U.S. forces gaining the upper hand. The Navy had held similar games involving a Pearl Harbor attack by enemy aircraft carriers as far back as 1933.

★★★★★

June 13, 1941: "The only real answer was for the fleet not to be in Pearl Harbor when the attack came." That statement was made by Admiral Kimmel (CINCUS), during a Washington meeting with Chief of Naval Operations Admiral Stark and Secretary of the Navy Knox. Kimmel had said the congestion of ships, fuel oil storage, and repair facilities in Pearl Harbor invited an "attack, particularly from the air." With the fleet in port it would take at least three hours to sortie, he noted.

★★★★★

June 1941: The United States government ordered all German and Italian consulates in the U.S. closed. Japan, as the third member of the Tripartite Pact, expected its consulates (including the one in Oahu), to also be closed. This eventuality caused concern among Admiral Yamamoto's superiors in the Imperial Japa-

nese Navy General Staff. They feared that such action would greatly limit Japanese espionage activities on the U.S. Fleet and thereby necessitate a cancellation of the Pearl Harbor attack. However, the U.S. never issued an order to close the Japanese consulates, and they continued to function up to the moment of the attack.

★★★★★

July 1941: Lieutenant Colonel Kendall (Wooch) Fielder became the intelligence officer (G-2) on the staff of General Short. Fielder had no prior intelligence duty and had not previously served under Short.

★★★★★

July 10, 1941: "Our most likely enemy, Orange, can probably employ a maximum of six carriers against Oahu. . . . The early morning attack is, therefore, the best plan of action to the enemy." This accurate statement was contained in a report submitted by Colonel William E. Farthing, commander of the Fifth Bombardment Group, Hickam Field, Oahu, Hawaii. The purpose of "the Farthing Report" was to analyze the use of bombardment aviation as a defense for Hawaii.

★★★★★

July 1941: A Gallup Poll reflected that 51 percent of the American population was willing to risk war with Japan. A second poll, taken in September, indicated that 70 percent held that attitude two months later.

★★★★★

August 12, 1941: "An attack upon these [Hawaiian] islands is not impossible and in certain situations might not be improbable." Excerpt from an address by General Short at the University of Hawaii.

Japan lost only 29 of the 432 planes that participated in the December 7 attack: five Nakajima B5N2 Kate high-level bombers, nine Mitsubishi A6M2 Zero-sen fighters, and 15 Aichi D3A2 Val dive bombers. The wreckage shown here is a Val, one of 51 in the first wave.

September 10, 1941: General Short made a strong request to the U.S. War Department for bombproof aircraft facilities, which he said would be "vital to the continued functioning of the Hawaiian Air Force during an attack on Oahu." The request was not received favorably.

★★★★★

September 20, 1941: Major General Martin, commander of the Hawaiian Air Force, submitted a plan calling for joint Army-Navy exercise drills to specifically train against a potential Japanese carrier-based air attack. Martin proposed that the war games take place November 17–22. At the time Martin made the request the Japanese were themselves considering November 16 or 23 as the date for the attack. Martin's request was not acted on favorably.

★★★★★

November 7, 1941: Secretary of State Cordell Hull, responding to a question from President Roosevelt at a cabinet meeting, stated: "Relations were extremely critical, and we should be on the lookout for a military attack anywhere by Japan at any time."

★★★★★

November 7, 1941: Exactly one month before the attack, Admiral Stark, CNO rejected another request from Admiral Kimmel that the battleships USS *North Carolina* and USS *Washington,* plus more destroyers, be sent to Pearl Harbor to join the fleet: "Things seem to be moving steadily toward crisis in the Pacific," Stark wrote, adding, "A month may see literally anything."

★★★★★

November 27, 1941: Washington sent what has become known as the "war warning" message to U.S. forces in the Pacific. It said in part: "An aggressive move by Japan is expected within the next few days."

December 1941: While at the office of U.S. Naval Intelligence in Washington, Captain Johan Ranneft, the Dutch naval attaché, was told that two Japanese aircraft carriers were proceeding east between Japan and Hawaii. He asked where they were, and an officer pointed to a wall map and indicated a position between 300 and 400 miles northwest of Honolulu. (NOTE: *This incident is one of several that authors Prange and Toland disagree about. Toland reports it as fact in* Infamy, *whereas Prange dismisses it in* Pearl Harbor: The Verdict of History.)

★★★★★

December 2, 1941: Lieutenant Ellsworth A. Hosner and another staff member of the 12th Naval District Intelligence Office (San Francisco) detected radio signals in the Pacific they thought could be from the Japanese fleet (which had been missing since late November). Their commander, Captain Richard T. McCullough, a friend of President Roosevelt, was advised. These two officers continued to track the signals and on December 6 correctly established that the position was about 400 miles north of Oahu.

★★★★★

December 2, 1941: When the passenger liner *Lurline* made port in Honolulu after a passage from California, her officers reported to the U.S. Navy that they had accidentally picked up a series of unidentifiable high-frequency transmissions from Tokyo and low-frequency replies from ships that they had plotted to be closing in on Hawaii.

★★★★★

December 2, 1941: "Do you mean to say that they [the Japanese fleet] could be rounding Diamond Head this minute and you wouldn't know?" Irritated question from Admiral Kimmel after his intelligence officer informed him that the Japanese carrier force that had left its home waters in late November was still "missing" to U.S. plotters.

The concept of adding wooden stabilizers to the fins of torpedoes carried by Japanese aircraft so that the weapons would not hit the 45-foot bottom of Pearl Harbor was the brainchild of Navy Commander Minoru Genda. It was the general opinion in U.S. Navy circles that the harbor was not deep enough for a torpedo-plane attack, as approximately a 70-foot depth was thought to be minimal for success. Genda went on to become a major general and chief of staff of the Japanese Air Self-Defense Force and later served as a member in the upper house of the Diet (the Japanese equivalent of the U.S. Senate).

—Author's collection

December 1941: General Hein Ter Poorten, commander of the Netherlands East Indies Army, advised the U.S. military observer in Java, Brigadier General Elliott Thorpe, in early December that Japan would attack Hawaii, the Philippines, Malaya, and Thailand shortly. He further noted that the signal for hostilities against the U.S. would be the message "East wind, rain," which U.S. code breakers had already found in a November 29 message from Tokyo to its ambassador in Washington. General Thorpe sent this information to Washington along with three other messages on the same subject. *Washington's reply requested he send no further information on the subject.*

★★★★★

December 6, 1941: Admiral Kimmel, in a meeting with aides, updated a memorandum titled "Steps to Be Taken in Case of American-Japanese War Within the Next Twenty-four Hours."

★★★★★

December 6, 1941: "They [Japan] will attack right here." The prophetic statement by Ensign Fred Hall, the assistant communications officer aboard the USS *Vestal* (AR-4), was interjected into a conversation among officers in the ship's wardroom. However, nobody bothered to ask Hall when the attack would take place. At 7:55 the following morning Hall was the officer of the deck and pulled what may have been the first general-quarters alarm on any ship in Pearl Harbor.

★★★★★

December 6, 1941: "The Japanese will not go to war with the United States. We are too big, too powerful, and too strong." Boast made by Vice Admiral William Satterlee Pye, the second-highest-ranking U.S. Navy officer at Pearl Harbor, to other officers on Oahu.

December 6, 1941: On seeing the U.S. Fleet all lit up in Pearl Harbor the evening before the attack, General Short exclaimed, "What a target that would make!" The general, his wife, and his intelligence officer, Lieutenant Colonel Fielder, were returning home after attending a party.

★★★★★

December 6, 1941: "This means war." Statement by President Roosevelt to his aide Harry Hopkins after reading the first 13 parts of the Tokyo message U.S. intelligence intercepted en route to the Japanese ambassadors in Washington.

★★★★★

December 6, 1941: "War is imminent. You may run into a war during your flight." Statement by Major General Henry H. (Hap) Arnold to members of the 38th and 88th Reconnaissance Squadrons, who were about to leave the U.S. to deliver several B-17s to the Philippines. Their flight plan called for a scheduled fuel stop at Oahu, Hawaii, around 8 A.M. on December 7.

★★★★★

December 6, 1941: "If we are going into a war, why don't we have machine guns?" Question to General Arnold from Major Truman H. Landon during the above briefing. To conserve fuel, the planes had been stripped of weaponry.

★★★★★

December 7, 1941: After reading the 14th and final part of the Japanese message and noting that the 1 P.M. deadline in the nation's capital would be 7:30 A.M. in Hawaii, three intelligence officers correctly concluded that it suggested the outbreak of hostilities against Pearl Harbor was nearly certain. The officers were U.S. Army Colonel Rufus S. Bratton, Commander Arthur H. McCollum, and Lieutenant Commander A. D. Kramer, both of Naval Intelligence.

The only battleship to get under way after the Pearl Harbor attack began was the USS Nevada *(BB-36). It normally took three hours, 30 minutes to get under way, but* Nevada *accomplished the task in 45 minutes.* Nevada *later saw action at Normandy and Iwo Jima. After the war it was used as a target ship in the 1946 atom bomb tests off Bikini Island but was not sunk until 1948, when it was a target ship in naval weapons tests. In the accompanying photo the* Nevada *is seen settling and burning after being beached at Waipio Point to prevent it from sinking in the channel entrance to Pearl Harbor.*

—*U.S. Navy photo*

December 7, 1941: "No, thanks, Betty, I feel I can get it through quickly enough." Reply from General Marshall to Admiral Stark's offer to send the following message, marked *First Priority—Secret* to Pearl Harbor:

The Japanese are presenting at 1 P.M. Eastern Standard Time today what amounts to an ultimatum. Also they are under orders to destroy their code machine immediately. Just what significance the hour set may have we do not know, but be on the alert accordingly.

After turning down Stark's offer to send the message via the Navy's rapid transmission system, Marshall had it sent, in code, via Western Union. Admiral Kimmel and General Short did not receive the decoded version until seven hours after the attack had begun.

★★★★★

December 7, 1941: "So sorry, we sank your fleet this morning. Supposing we are at war?" Comment by a Japanese newsman to C. L. Sulzberger of the *New York Times* during an encounter at the Grand Hotel in Moscow.

★★★★★

December 7, 1941: "How did they catch us with our pants down, Mr. President?" The question that was being asked in homes throughout America was first put to President Roosevelt by Senator Thomas Connally (D-Tex.) on the evening of the attack during a meeting with cabinet and congressional leaders.

★★★★★

TIME HAD RUN OUT

The first published account of a Japanese surprise attack on the U.S. fleet based at Pearl Harbor appeared in print in 1925, 16 years before the Day of Infamy. Author Hector C. Bywater detailed a fictitious surprise attack in his novel *The Great Pacific War*. The book was reportedly used in the Japanese Navy War College. In addition, more than one Japanese novelist used the theme of attacking Pearl Harbor in the years that followed.

★★★★★

The first contact U.S. naval forces operating out of Pearl Harbor had with Japanese ships that would be involved in the Pearl Harbor attack on December 7 actually came two days earlier. On December 5, the destroyers USS *Selfridge* (DD-357) and USS *Ralph Talbot* (DD-390) made underwater contact with what the *Talbot* commander reported as a submarine about five miles off Pearl Harbor. He requested permission to depth-charge but was denied such authority by his land-based superiors with the explanation that the readings he was getting were more probably from a blackfish than a sub. "If this is a blackfish, it has a motorboat up its stern!" he reportedly responded. That same night Admiral William F. Halsey's task force was advised that a submarine had been reported on December 4 just south of Hawaii.

★★★★★

The first *un*official word of the Pearl Harbor attack was transmitted on the only commercial cable line linking Hawaii to the mainland by United Press International's Honolulu Bureau Chief Frank Tremaine at 10:30 A.M. PST, on December 7, 1941. It was received at UPI's San Francisco office by the weekend bureau chief James Sullivan who flagged the cable "FLASH" (highest priority) and transcribed it to the news agency's main office in New York. Tremaine watched the attack from his house overlooking the harbor. He shouted what he was witnessing to his wife Kay who

The USS Phoenix (CL-46), a light cruiser, was the last ship present at Pearl Harbor on December 7, 1941, later to be sunk by enemy action. In 1951 the U.S. Navy sold the Phoenix to Argentina, who renamed her the General Belgrano. She was torpedoed by a British submarine off the Falkland Islands on May 2, 1982. In this U.S. Navy photo she is seen burning following the December 7 attack.

—U.S. Navy photos

146

In this February 28, 1944 photo by Pfc. Gae Falilace, Vice Admiral Thomas C. Kinkaid and General Douglas MacArthur observe the bombardment of Los Negros Island from the flag bridge of the Phoenix. Colonel Lloyd Labarbas, an aide to MacArthur, is at extreme right.

—U.S. Navy photos

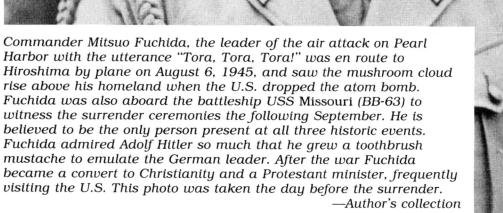

Commander Mitsuo Fuchida, the leader of the air attack on Pearl Harbor with the utterance "Tora, Tora, Tora!" was en route to Hiroshima by plane on August 6, 1945, and saw the mushroom cloud rise above his homeland when the U.S. dropped the atom bomb. Fuchida was also aboard the battleship USS Missouri (BB-63) to witness the surrender ceremonies the following September. He is believed to be the only person present at all three historic events. Fuchida admired Adolf Hitler so much that he grew a toothbrush mustache to emulate the German leader. After the war Fuchida became a convert to Christianity and a Protestant minister, frequently visiting the U.S. This photo was taken the day before the surrender.
—Author's collection

The last Japanese pilot to return to the carrier force was Commander Mitsuo Fuchida, whose "Tora! Tora! Tora!" message back to the Japanese fleet at 7:53 A.M. indicated that complete surprise had been achieved as the attack began. Fuchida continued to circle Oahu and evaluate damage even after the second wave had finished. He returned to the *Akagi* at approximately 1 P.M. and unsuccessfully pleaded with Admiral Nagumo for a second attack. The Japanese fleet began to withdraw from the area at 1:30 P.M. The flag that had flown on the *Akagi* during the attack was the same one that had flown on Admiral Heihachiro Togo's ship in the 1905 Japanese victory over the Russians.

★★★★★

The first message to the outside world concerning the attack is widely credited as having been authorized by Rear Admiral Patrick Bellinger at 7:58 A.M. It was simple and to the point: "Air raid, Pearl Harbor. This is no drill." Bellinger is named as the officer who sent the message in Samuel Eliot Morison's *The Two–Ocean War;* Walter Lord's *Day of Infamy;* Lieutenant Colonel Eddy Bauer's 24-volume *Illustrated World War II Encyclopedia;* and various other accounts. However, in *At Dawn We Slept,* Gordon Prange credits Lieutenant Commander Logan Ramsey as the sender, also at 7:58. In this version "no drill" is replaced by "not drill." It is interesting to note that Ramsey was with a Lieutenant Richard Ballinger near the radio room of the Ford Island command center at this point in the attack and reportedly ran into the room to order radiomen on duty to send out the message. There were at least two other messages, similar in content, sent over the air in the immediate minutes reported here.

★★★★★

The first combat between pilots from American and Japanese aircraft carriers took place during the December 7 attack. The USS *Enterprise* (CV-6) and USS *Lexington* (CV-2) were returning to Pearl Harbor after ferrying planes to Midway and Wake islands. However, *Enterprise,* due back at 7:30, had experienced re-

fueling problems and was approximately 200 miles west of Oahu. Eighteen aircraft from *Enterprise* left the carrier and reached Pearl Harbor at 8 A.M. during the attack. Their radio messages of what was going on were picked up by *Enterprise,* which, observing radio

silence, turned course and vanished deeper into the Pacific. Admiral Halsey, on seeing the devastation when the *Enterprise* returned, commented: "Before we're through with 'em, the Japanese language will be spoken only in hell."

The first prisoner of war captured by the U.S. was Ensign Kazuo Sakamaki, commander of a Japanese midget submarine involved in the attack on Pearl Harbor. Sakamaki was taken prisoner by U.S. Army Sargeant David M. Akui, who found the hapless submariner unconscious on the beach near the Kanoehe-Bellows Field area of Oahu late in the evening of the attack. Unable to scuttle his boat after experiencing mechanical difficulties (from being depth-charged by the USS Helm [DD-388]) and weakened by exhaustion, Sakamaki and a second officer abandoned the sub and attempted to make their way ashore. Sakamaki succeeded and then passed out. He awoke to find Sargeant Akui standing over him. No trace of his companion was ever found. The first photo shows one of the Japanese two-man subs beached on a small island off Oahu. The second photo is of another midget sub on exhibit at Bellows Field, Oahu, Hawaii.

—U.S. Navy photo

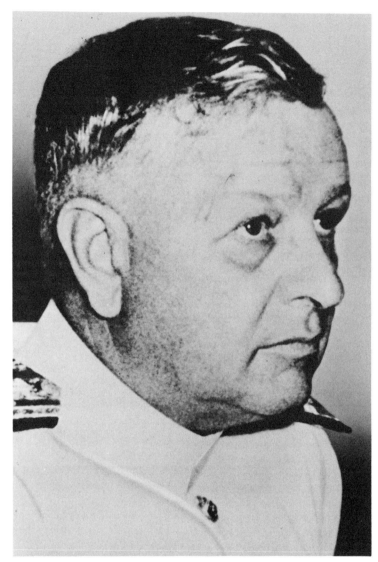

February 1, 1941: Admiral Husband E. Kimmel, began his tour of duty as Commander in Chief, U.S. Fleet, at Pearl Harbor.

The new Army commander on Oahu, General Walter C. Short, would assume his duties a week later, on February 7.

—U.S. Navy photos

The first ship sunk at Pearl Harbor on December 7 was not a U.S. warship but a Japanese midget sub that had been sighted by a Catalina flying boat. Its location was transmitted to Lieutenant William W. Outerbridge, commanding the destroyer USS *Ward* (DD-139) which was patrolling the waters outside Pearl Harbor. The *Ward* depth-charged and sank the sub at 6:45 A.M., more than an hour before the attack. A second sub was sighted and sunk at 7 A.M. by a Catalina flying boat. The sub sunk by the *Ward* was later identified as the one that had initially been reported by the *Condor* (AMc-14).

★★★★★

The first Japanese ship captured by the U.S. Navy was a sampan in the restricted area of Pearl Harbor, one hour before the attack began.

★★★★★

The first U.S. sighting of Japanese planes en route to attack Pearl Harbor came nearly an hour before the attack. U.S. Army privates Joseph L. Lockard and George E. Elliott were scheduled to go off duty at the Opana Mobile Radar Station on Oahu at 7 A.M. the morning of December 7. However, a short time before closing down their operation, they observed an unusual blip on the screen and determined it was a group of planes heading for Oahu. Intrigued, they decided to remain beyond the end of their shift to watch and report it to Lieutenant Kermit Tyler, the pursuit officer on duty at the Army's Information Center. Tyler had the authority to sound an alert and authorize U.S. sorties to "intercept enemy planes." However, he believed the blip Lockard and Elliott were reporting was an expected flight of B-17s and ignored it. The two Army privates watched the blip for several more minutes before finally closing down their station and leaving. Unbeknownst to them at the time, they had observed the first wave of Japanese planes nearly an hour before the attack began.

The only U.S. warship that was present at both the Pearl Harbor attack on December 7, 1941, and the Normandy invasion on D-Day, June 6, 1944, was the battleship USS *Nevada* (BB-36).

★★★★★

Contrary to widely held belief after the Pearl Harbor attack, the U.S. Navy was *not* wiped out. There were 145 Navy and Coast Guard ships present, but only 18 of the 96 *warships* were sunk. Ships in the Atlantic and elsewhere were obviously not affected: all six aircraft carriers, 112 submarines, and eight light cruisers were intact; three of the Navy's 18 heavy cruisers had been at Pearl, but none were damaged; and only three out of 171 destroyers had been at Pearl.

★★★★★

The last ship to sortie in Pearl Harbor on December 7 was the cruiser USS *St. Louis* (CL-49), which ran at 22 knots in an eight-knot zone in order to clear the channel at 10:04 A.M. The *St. Louis* immediately had to take evasive action to avoid two torpedoes fired from a Japanese midget submarine. The fish struck the coral reef near the channel entrance. The *St. Louis* returned fire and reported that it had hit the coning tower.

★★★★★

The two newest of the six Japanese aircraft carriers that participated in the Pearl Harbor attack were the *Shokaku* and *Zuikaku*, both of which entered service in the summer of 1941. *Shokaku* was sunk by an American submarine in the Philippine Sea on June 19, 1944, and *Zuikaku* went to the bottom on October 25, 1944, as a result of U.S. carrier-borne aircraft fire during the Battle of Leyte Gulf. *Akagi*, the flagship for the Pearl Harbor attack force, had been launched in 1925, and along with the other three carriers that had been at Pearl Harbor, *Kaga, Hiryu,* and *Soryu*, was sunk on June 4 and 5 during the Battle of Midway.

U.S. servicemen killed during the Pearl Harbor attack were laid to rest together.

—U.S. Navy photo

The little-known *second* Japanese attack on Pearl Harbor occurred on the evening of March 3, 1942, less than three months after the "Day of Infamy." Two Japanese Emily bombers (Kawanishi H8K2 flying boats) based in the Marshall Islands and refueled by submarine attacked Hawaii. The bombs from one plane missed land altogether and fell into the Pacific. The second plane got disoriented in the clouds and bombed Mt. Tantalus instead of Pearl Harbor. There were no casualties.

★★★★★

The most difficult of all the salvage operations taken in the aftermath of the Pearl Harbor attack was the raising of the minelayer USS *Oglala* (CM-4), despite the fact she was not nearly as large as the several battleships or a number of the other ships sunk. *Oglala*, which was 34 years old, and the cruiser USS *Helena* (CL-50) were moored together on Battleship Row in the berth usually occupied by the USS *Pennsylvania* (BB-38). *Oglala* had not been designed as a warship or compartmentalized, and as a result she literally burst at the seams from concussion when a torpedo passed under her and hit the *Helena* at 7:57 A.M. Salvors would later say *Oglala* died of fright. The lack of a strong internal structure made raising her tedious, long, and difficult.

★★★★★

The first antiaircraft fire of any significance from the American fleet did not begin until 10 minutes after the Japanese attack began.

★★★★★

The oldest officer on active duty with the Imperial Japanese Navy at the time of the attack was the 62-year-old chief of the naval general staff, Admiral Osami Nagano. During a distinguished career he had studied at Harvard and served as naval attaché in Washington, and he considered New York City his second home.

The first person to sight the Japanese at Pearl Harbor was Ensign R. C. McCloy, officer of the deck aboard the minesweeper USS *Condor* (AMc-14), which along with the USS *Crossbill* was operating about one-and-three-quarter miles south of the harbor's entrance. At 3:42 A.M. McCloy spotted what he believed was a periscope some "fifty yards ahead off the port bow" and asked Quartermaster Second Class R. C. Uttrick to use the binoculars and report what he saw. "That's a periscope, sir, and there aren't supposed to be any subs in this area," the sailor responded. At 3:57 McCloy sent a blinker message to the destroyer USS *Ward* (DD-139), which was on channel entrance patrol: "Sighted submerged submarine on westerly course, speed nine knots." *Ward* went to general quarters and asked *Condor* for an update on the sub's position. *Condor* responded that its last sighting was at 3:50 A.M. and the sub appeared to be heading for the harbor entrance. *Ward* searched unsuccessfully for the sub until 4:35. At 4:58 the antisubmarine nets at the harbor entrance were opened to admit the *Condor* and *Crossbill.* Neither *Condor* nor *Ward* reported the sighting to Pearl Harbor. The sub nets wouldn't be closed until 8:40 A.M., almost an hour after the attack began.

★★★★★

The only U.S. Navy submariner wounded during the attack on Pearl Harbor was Seaman 2nd Class G. A. Myers, who was hit by Japanese aircraft fire while aboard the USS *Cachalot* (SS-170).

★★★★★

The attack on Pearl Harbor and other U.S. installations on Oahu was the largest aircraft carrier operation carried out up till that time.

★★★★★

Nearly half of the 2,403 Americans killed in the attack were aboard the USS *Arizona.*

Lieutenant Fusata Iida, leader of a group of Zero fighters from the Soryu, was buried with honor by U.S. military personnel on Oahu. —U.S. Navy photo

In terms of human life Japan lost 55 fliers, nine midget submariners (plus one captured), and an unknown number aboard an I-class submarine in the Pearl Harbor attack. Lieutenant Fusata Iida, leader of a Japanese fighter group in the second wave, lost his life in a remarkable shootout at Kaneohe Naval Air Station. While addressing pilots of the nine Zeros that would follow him from the carrier *Soryu,* Iida asked, "What are you going to do in case you have engine trouble in flight?" Before he received an answer, he told his audience what he himself intended to do: "In case of trouble I will fly straight to my objective and make a crash dive into an enemy target rather than make an emergency landing." He remained true to his word, but with a little help from an aviation ordnanceman. As the *Soryu* fighter group was attacking Kaneohe, Iida came in low and riddled the station's armory. Suddenly a lone sailor came into clear view firing a Browning Automatic Rifle (BAR) directly at him. The Zero, guns blazing, passed over the sailor's head practically at rooftop level. Iida banked, turned, and headed back toward the armory as the sailor changed clips. Iida began his second run. Other servicemen in the area found themselves frozen in disbelief as they watched this seemingly unequal battle: the Zero pilot and the lone sailor on the ground pumped rounds at each other, head on. Again the Zero flashed over the sailor's head, but this time it appeared to be flying away and rejoining its group. Suddenly other pilots noticed fuel gushing from Iida's tanks. They knew his chances of making it back to the *Soryu* were not very good.

As the planes closest to him watched, Iida patted himself on the chest and then pointed toward the ground. They understood immediately what he meant and what he was going to do. As Iida swung around and began heading back toward the armory, the sailor who had been firing the BAR was still in the open near the building, but this time he had a rifle. Iida aimed directly for him and opened up with all he had. The sailor, bullets ripping into the ground all around him, emptied the rifle at the Zero. Iida's guns stopped abruptly a few seconds before he passed over the sailor for the last time. His plane hit the ground, skidded, and tumbled to a halt. Of the 33 PBYs at Kaneohe Naval Air Station, Iida's planes totally destroyed 27 and damaged the other six. Three others escaped destruction by being on patrol at the time.

★★★★★

The first U.S. Navy pilot killed in action was Ensign Manuel Gonzalez, one of the USS *Enterprise* (CV-6) pilots who flew into the Pearl Harbor attack. That evening four dive bombers from the *Enterprise* were shot down by friendly fire while trying to land on Oahu. They had landed on the island earlier in the day but were sent out to search for the Japanese fleet. Returning in the dark, they were mistaken for enemy planes.

★★★★★

Only 38 of the 390 U.S. military aircraft on Oahu were able to sortie once the attack began. Of them 10 were shot down.

★★★★★

The highest-ranking U.S. naval officer killed in the war was Rear Admiral Isaac C. Kidd, who was mortally wounded while manning a machine gun aboard his flagship, the USS *Arizona* (BB-39), during the attack on Pearl Harbor. Every rank in the U.S. Navy is represented by the more than 1,100 men entombed in the *Arizona.*

★★★★★

The first black American to receive a Navy Cross in the war was Mess Attendant 2nd Class Doris Miller for action aboard the battleship USS *West Virginia* on December 7, 1941. Although untrained with the weapon, Miller manned an idle machine gun during the Japanese attack on Pearl Harbor and, according to his citation, displayed courage, coolness, and initiative. Miller, who was West Virginia's heavyweight boxing champion, received the award from Admiral Chester W. Nimitz on May 27, 1942.

The USS Arizona as she appeared in 1918, three years after going into service. She is seen here departing New York harbor as part of President Woodrow Wilson's honor escort to the Paris Peace conference.

—U.S. Navy photo

★★★★★

Ironies

★★★★★

The American opinion of the Japanese prior to, and even after, Pearl Harbor saw them as a backward, ignorant race while the media made much of the fact that in Europe a number of German generals had studied at Oxford and other leading English schools before the war. However, it was not commonly known that several leading Japanese naval officers had attended some of the finest universities and colleges in the U.S. Among the Ivy League alumni in the Imperial Japanese Navy who planned or participated in the December 7 attack were

Admiral Osami Nagano	Harvard
Fleet Admiral Isoroku Yamamoto	Harvard
Rear Admiral Tamon Yamaguchi	Princeton
Captain Takayasu Arima	Yale

★★★★★

Less than a month after Japanese Admiral Yamamoto first privately discussed the idea of attacking the U.S. fleet at Pearl Harbor the *Honolulu Advertiser* carried the following quote in its pages: "If there were ever men and a fleet ready for any emergency, it's Uncle Sam's fighting ships."

★★★★★

Joseph C. Grew, the U.S. ambassador to Japan for nearly a decade at the time of the attack on Pearl Harbor, was partially deaf and had never managed to master the Japanese language. However, his wife, Alice, the granddaughter of Commodore Perry, spoke the tongue fluently.

The U.S. Navy had 17 seaworthy battleships prior to the Pearl Harbor attack, nine of which were in the Pacific (the USS *Colorado* [BB-45] was in the naval dockyard at Bremerton, Washington). Of the five sunk and three damaged at Pearl Harbor, only two, the USS *Arizona* (BB-39) and USS *Oklahoma* (BB-37), were completely lost.

★★★★★

The first woman to receive a Purple Heart in the war was U.S. Army nurse Ann Fox for injuries she sustained during the Japanese attack on Hickam Field.

★★★★★

Because of the Americans' ability to read the Japanese diplomatic and other codes, U.S. intelligence personnel were alerted to watch for the phrase *Higashi no kazeame* (East wind, rain), which could be expected to be buried in an otherwise normal-sounding communication from Tokyo. The significance of the phrase would be to inform Japanese diplomats that relations with the U.S. were in danger. As noted elsewhere in this section, Japanese Ambassador Nomura received a message from the Foreign Office in Tokyo on November 29, 1941, in which U.S. code breakers found the phrase "East wind, rain."

★★★★★

The reason the U.S. fleet was at anchor in Pearl Harbor rather than out at sea was due to a critical fuel shortage. Admiral Kimmel wanted to keep two task forces at sea at all times while only one remained in port. However, all fuel for the fleet had to be brought to Hawaii from the U.S. mainland, and only four of the Pacific fleet's tankers were capable of fueling ships at sea. As an example of fuel consumption, a single destroyer at sea was capable of consuming its entire fuel supply in 30 hours.

Although the Japanese attack on Pearl Harbor and elsewhere on Oahu was confined to military installations, the city of Honolulu was rocked by upward of 40 explosions and sustained approximately $500,000 worth of damage. But the destruction was caused by U.S. antiaircraft fire, not Japanese pilots.

—U.S. Army photo

★★★★★

The U.S. fleet that was to come under attack at Pearl Harbor left the U.S. West Coast for maneuvers around Hawaii on April 2, 1940. A little more than a month later, on May 7, President Roosevelt ordered the fleet to remain in Hawaii indefinitely.

★★★★★

The only U.S. aerial photographs taken of the Japanese attack on Pearl Harbor were made by Staff Sergeant Lee Embree aboard one of the twelve B-17 bombers that were arriving from California. Thinking the large camera he swung out of a hatch was a gun, Japanese planes avoided his particular B-17.

★★★★★

In the Buddhist fortune calendar cycle of 12 years, 1941 was the Year of the Snake. Though no connection with the evil disposition of the reptile and the ambitions of Japan was made in the empire, it was quickly seized on by Allied propagandists after December 7.

Kiichi Gunji, the Japanese consul general based in Hawaii, got a good deal of the information he sent to Japan about movements of the U.S. fleet from the pages of local newspapers. As a service to military families, newspapers regularly printed the exact arrival and departure times of fleet ships. Though public information in Hawaii, this information became classified the moment it arrived in Japan. Kohichi Seki, the Japanese consulate's treasurer, used a copy of *Jane's Fighting Ships* to identify vessels of the fleet that he observed as he scouted Pearl Harbor during casual drives.

★★★★★

Aerial photos of Pearl Harbor and Hickam Field were obtained by members of the Japanese consulate who took private sightseeing plane rides from John Rogers Airport, an activity duplicated hundreds of times by ordinary tourists before the war.

★★★★★

The Japanese military officer who scouted the naval operations at Pearl Harbor was Lieutenant Commander Suguru Suzuki. He arrived in Oahu in October 1941 as a passenger aboard the *Taiyo Maru* out of Japan.

★★★★★

In 1928 during U.S. Navy "Fleet Problem VIII," planes from America's first aircraft carrier, USS *Langley*, executed a successful surprise "attack" against the Army garrison and naval defenders at Pearl Harbor.

★★★★★

In a U.S. Navy war games exercise in 1939, aircraft from the carrier USS *Saratoga* (CV-3) succeeded in a Sunday morning surprise attack on Pearl Harbor and other military installations on Oahu. The attacking aircraft "sank" several ships at anchor in Pearl Harbor and attacked Hickam, Wheeler, and Ford Island airfields before returning safely to their carrier.

★★★★★

As the Japanese attack force left home waters and began heading for Hawaii, their intelligence reports told them all six of the big American aircraft carriers would be with the fleet at Pearl Harbor. This was incorrect. The USS *Langley* (CV-1) was in the Atlantic, and the other five had been in the Pacific until USS *Yorktown* (CV-5) and USS *Hornet* (CV-8) joined the *Langley* there. USS *Saratoga* (CV-3), meanwhile, was close to the West Coast, leaving only two carriers, USS *Enterprise* (CV-6) and USS *Lexington* (CV-2). And neither of them would be in port when the attack came. The *Enterprise* was ferrying aircraft to Wake Island and the *Lexington* was doing the same to Midway.

★★★★★

In telephone calls between Tokyo and its embassy staff in Washington during the negotiations prior to Pearl Harbor, President Roosevelt was referred to as *Miss Kimiko* and Secretary of State Hull as *Miss Fumeko*. The United States was *Minami* and the U.S. Army was called *Tokugawa*. By introducing these and other code names into seemingly innocuous telephone conversations, the Japanese Foreign Ministry was able to get an instant reading from its ambassadors as to the progress of the peace talks.

★★★★★

The name the Imperial Japanese Navy gave to its formidable Pearl Harbor strike force, and used to identify it in communications, was Kido Butai. Various translations describe this as: a mechanized military force; an armed mobile unit; or the vanguard or strike force of an attack. There is no literal translation of Kido Butai to English.

The last U.S. Navy ship hit by Japanese gunfire in the war was the battleship USS Pennsylvania *(BB-38) on August 12, 1945, two days before the war ended. The* Pennsylvania *had also been the last battleship hit during the attack on Pearl Harbor. It is seen here in January 1945 entering the Lingayen Gulf preceding the landing of Luzon in the Philippines at the head of a column that included the USS* Colorado *(BB-45), USS* Louisville *(CA-28), USS* Portland *(CA-33), and USS* Columbia *(CL-56).*

—*U.S. Navy photo*

Contrary to facts, Japan continued to report through the spring of 1942 that the USS *Arizona* (BB-39) was sunk by one of its midget submarines. However, Japanese Petty Officer Noboru Kanai, regarded as the top horizontal bombardier in the Imperial Navy, is believed to have dropped the bomb that sank the battleship. Experts disagree, though, as to whether the bomb actually went down the smokestack (widely reported and popularly believed) or simply struck the ship in a vulnerable position. Kanai lost his life during the battle for Wake Island.

★★★★★

Prior to 1941, Japan had never had a navy fighter plane involved in action more than 100 miles from its home base or aircraft carrier because their radiotelephone communications system was unable to function beyond that distance. Therefore, throughout the summer of 1941 Japanese navy pilots and communications personnel had to become proficient in Morse code in order to sustain communications during the planned attack on Pearl Harbor. After the attack, the Japanese fleet returned to the port of Hiroshima.

★★★★★

Admiral Husband E. Kimmel failed to gain admission to West Point, his first choice when applying to military academies. He then applied to Annapolis, much to the chagrin of his family, which had a West Point tradition, and graduated 13th in a class of 62. In the early days of his career (circa 1913) Kimmel served briefly as an aide to then Assistant Secretary of the Navy Franklin D. Roosevelt.

★★★★★

The most prestigious command in the U.S. Navy, prior to December 7, 1941, was Commander in Chief, U.S. Fleet (CINCUS), based in Pearl Harbor. The title was later changed to Commander in Chief, Pacific (CINC-PAC), after several bad jokes about the phonetics of CINCUS (sink us) having been an invitation to Japan. Ten months before the attack Admiral Kimmel had been promoted to CINCUS over the heads of 32 more senior admirals. He was fired 10 days after the attack.

★★★★★

The two leading air officers in the Japanese attack on Pearl Harbor wore red underwear and red shirts in order to conceal any injuries they might sustain during the raid. Flight Leader Mitsuo Fuchida, the overall attack commander, and Lieutenant Commander Shigemaru Murata, leader of the torpedo bombers in the first wave, reasoned that if they became wounded, their blood would not show up against the red. Their intention was to prevent demoralizing other flying officers.

★★★★★

Japan's official announcement that a state of war existed with the U.S. (and the British Empire) was not made until three hours after the attack was finished.

★★★★★

In addition to reading the Japanese Purple code, the U.S. had broken and was reading the lower-grade "J codes" between the Foreign Ministry and several of its consulates, including Hawaii, since the summer of 1940. The significance of this is that from one code, J-19, the U.S. was fully aware of Tokyo's interest in the position and/or movement of the U.S. fleet based in Hawaii. Interestingly, Nazi Heinrich Stahmer, the man who had negotiated the Tripartite Pact in Tokyo, told the Japanese in May 1941 that Germany had evidence the U.S. was reading their code messages. Japan found this impossible to believe and therefore did not change the codes. A few days before the December 7 attack, however, the Japanese consulate in Hawaii began using another code.

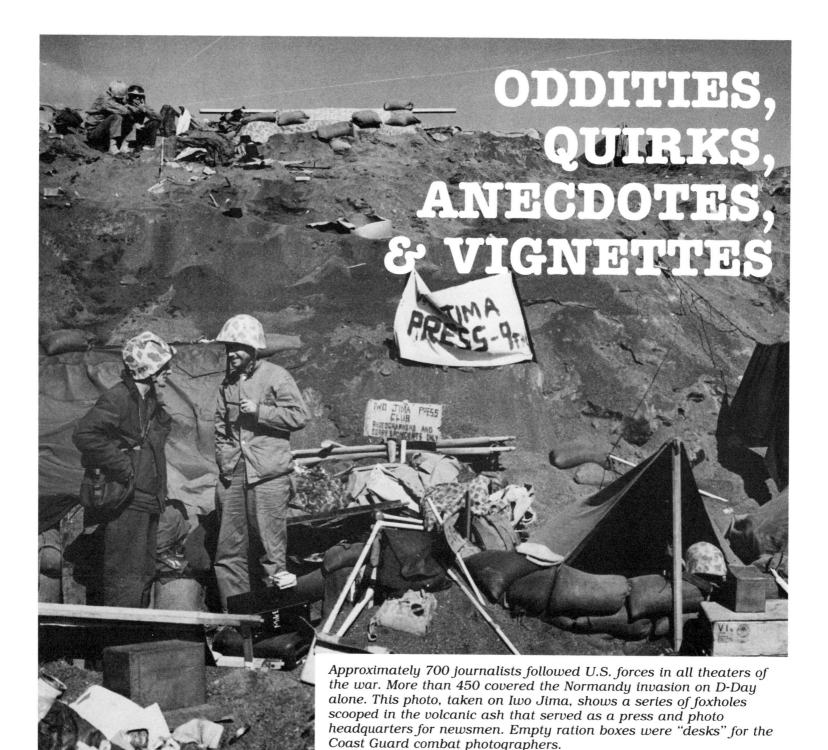

ODDITIES, QUIRKS, ANECDOTES, & VIGNETTES

Approximately 700 journalists followed U.S. forces in all theaters of the war. More than 450 covered the Normandy invasion on D-Day alone. This photo, taken on Iwo Jima, shows a series of foxholes scooped in the volcanic ash that served as a press and photo headquarters for newsmen. Empty ration boxes were "desks" for the Coast Guard combat photographers.

—U.S. Coast Guard photo

Revenge Is Sweet, and Sometimes a Little Weird

The most bizarre episode of revenge recorded by either side in the war involved an American pilot who sought out and shot down an Italian pilot who had shot him down. The Italian pilot, Guido Rossi, was flying an American P-38 and using the same tactics the Germans used in their KG 200 operations. The incident in question began when Rossi, in his decoy P-38, infiltrated a flight of B-17s and shot down one flown by U.S. Army Air Force Lieutenant Harold Fisher. The tactic bothered Fisher so much that he went out of his way learn the name of his nemesis, equip another B-17 with additional armament, and use himself to bait Rossi. When Fisher learned that Rossi's wife was behind Allied lines, he had her name and likeness painted on the plane's nose. A short time after Fisher began this highly unusual operation, he succeeded in attracting Rossi in his "friendly" P-38 again. During a chatty air-to-air conversation Fisher told Rossi that he had named the B-17 after the Italian woman he was living with, and then identified her. The ploy had the intended results. Rossi put his previous tactics aside and came at the B-17 straight on. Fisher shot him down, and Rossi was picked up as a prisoner of war. Fisher was awarded the Distinguished Flying Cross.

Sounds Like a Real Fun Guy

When Britain's Bernard Law Montgomery, who neither drank nor smoked, was a young officer, he advocated celibacy as a proper course for those who intended to pursue a military career.

Three Cheers for Tojo!

When the Marines reoccupied Guam, they discovered an unexpected but delightful surprise. The island had been the Japanese main liquor distribution center for the Central Pacific. Scotch, beer, bourbon, rye, and sake had been left behind for the leathernecks in great amounts.

But the Army Hit the Jackpot

When the U.S. 90th Division captured the city of Merkers, Germany, in April 1945, they discovered art, gold, and other valuables buried in the nearby salt mine. Much of the loot was Nazi plunder from occupied countries.

Right Church, Wrong Pew

Rommel and his army were surrounded by *German* troops on September 15, 1939, and ordered to surrender. However, the Rommel in question was not the German general and later field marshall, but rather Polish General Juliusz Rommel, the military commander of Warsaw.

Diplomatic Niceties

The only neutral country to have an official mourning period to mark the death of Adolf Hitler was Portugal. Following diplomatic protocol for the death of a head of state, flags were flown at half-staff on April 30 and May 1, 1945. Ireland stopped just short of lowering its flags, but Prime Minister Eamon de Valera actually expressed his condolences to German representatives in Dublin on May 2.

Hanky-Panky in the Third Reich

Adolf Hitler married his mistress, Eva Braun, shortly before they took their own lives. However, no fewer than five other infamous Naźis had mistresses. Josef Goebbels' mistress was Lida Baarova, but when the propaganda minister ended his life, it was in the company of his wife, Magda. The other four and their women: Heinrich Himmler and Hedwig Potthast; Martin Bormann and Manja Behrens; Dr. Josef Mengele and Irma Griese; Adolf Eichmann and Maria Masenbucher.

—*Berlin Senate Archives photo*

The Berlin Zoo Bunker

Because of Allied air attacks on Berlin the Germans built six massive bombproof bunkers around the city in 1941–42. The largest, near the zoo's bird sanctuary, rose 132 feet high, the approximate height of a 13-story building, and covered the equivalent space of a city block. It served as an antiaircraft complex, with eight five-inch guns and a number of pom-pom cannons on the roof; a 95-bed hospital with two fully equipped operating rooms, six doctors, and 50 nurses and orderlies; a warehouse for nearly all of the art treasures from Berlin's museums; and an air raid shelter that could accommodate 15,000 people. Self-contained, the bunker had its own power ,and water supply, and its kitchens were said to be so well stocked its defenders boasted they could survive for a year without being resupplied. Bunker walls were reinforced concrete more than eight feet thick, and its "windows" could be sealed by four-inch-thick steel plates. From 1942 on the Zoo Bunker was home to a permanent 100-man military garrison. As the Soviets entered Berlin, the Zoo Bunker became the last refuge for upward of 30,000 people.

This bunker, photographed in 1990, is one of two that were built in Hamburg and were identical to the Zoo Bunker in Berlin. After the war the other Hamburg bunker was demolished with great difficulty and expense. As a result it was determined to let this one remain. Today it houses a television and communications center.

—Photo by author

Hitler created the Mutterkreuz (Mother's Cross) for German women who gave birth to future little Nazis. Awarded in bronze, silver, and gold, depending on the number of children born, the Mutterkreuz was an amalgam of the Iron Cross, the Nazi Party Badge, and the Pour le Mérite. They were given out each year on the anniversary of Hitler's mother's birth, August 12. To earn the prestigious gold version required having eight or more children. Initiated in 1938, it was intended to honor women much in the same way soldiers earned citations for exceptional service.

—U.S. Army photo

How Schicklgruber Became Hitler

In a widely circulated story during the war, a U.S. Navy sailor named William Hitler reportedly changed his name before returning home. In one version the sailor is said to have been a relative of the German führer. This doesn't take into account that Adolf Hitler's father's name had been Alois Schicklgruber until it was changed in 1876. Adolf Hitler was the third son of the third marriage of his father, Alois, who had been an illegitimate child. For the first 39 years of his life Alois used his mother Maria Anna's family name, Schicklgruber. Adolf's parents were second cousins. Adolf's paternal grandfather was believed to have been Johann Heidler, who by 1876 had changed his name to Johann Hitler and swore under oath that he was the father of Alois Schicklgruber. There is evidence to suggest the only reason Heidler changed his name to Hitler was to collect an inheritance. Nonetheless, church baptismal records were changed and from that time on, 1876, Alois Schicklgruber (Adolf's father) legally became Alois Hitler. Thirteen years later on April 20, 1889, Alois had a son whom he named Adolf. Young Adolf once told his childhood friend August Kubizek that nothing had pleased him more than the fact that his father had changed the family name to Hitler. He considered Schicklgruber uncouth and boorish besides being clumsy and unpractical. He thought Heidler sounded too soft but, Adolf mused, Hitler "sounded nice and was easy to remember."

Author, Author, Führer, Führer

Adolf Hitler became a millionaire as a result of the royalties he earned from *Mein Kampf*. The first part of the book was written while he was in Landsberg Prison in 1925, but he added considerably more afterward. Once he came to power in 1933, Hitler arranged for copies to be given to newlyweds in the Reich, and it was this widespread distribution that increased his wealth.

We Love the Führer, But . . .

Much has been written about the Japanese kamikaze pilots who committed suicide to express their devotion and willingness to die for their emperor. Japanese kamikazes were responsible for sinking or damaging more than 300 U.S. Navy ships and causing approximately 15,000 casualties in the war. However, the Germans also employed suicide planes, of a sort. The main difference between the pilots for the two Axis countries was that the Japanese did not expect to return from their missions while the German *Sonderkommando Elbe* pilots did. The Germans had the option to parachute to safety if appropriate. In all, Germany mustered approximately 300 volunteers, mostly from the Luftwaffe, for its suicide force. Their first action, on April 7, 1945, was against Allied bombers, which they crashed into in midair. It followed by one day the first concentrated kamikaze action by the Japanese at Okinawa.

First an Iceberg, Then the Luftwaffe

Commander C. H. Lightoller, Royal Navy Reserve, was one of the most distinguished participants in the Dunkirk evacuation and rescue. He was the senior surviving officer of the *Titanic* and had been the major witness in the investigation of that disaster.

Return to Sender

The Japanese had presented "Good Friendship" medals to various American citizens in the years prior to the attack on Pearl Harbor. After December 7, 1941, several recipients decided to give them back, and return them they did, courtesy of Lieutenant Colonel Jimmy Doolittle. In a bogus ceremony before his squadron of B-25s lifted off the deck of the USS *Hornet* (CV-8), Doolittle, to the delight of his crews, attached the medals to bombs the planes would carry and drop on Japan.

On the eve of the liberation of Paris, Reichsführer Heinrich Himmler ordered a squad of SS to remove a particular tapestry from the Louvre. Created nine centuries earlier for William the Conqueror, it depicted the invasion of England. Since the Nazi plan to invade England (Operation Sea Lion) had never come to pass, Himmler thought the tapestry would be appreciated by Hitler. The SS squad was unable to get the tapestry because of heavy fire from members of the Resistance. In the accompanying photo Himmler is seen congratulating Hitler on the Führer's penultimate birthday, April 20, 1944. The others are, from left: Field Marshall Keitel, Admiral Doenitz, and Field Marshall Milch.

—Ullstein photo

Heil . . . Ugh? Heil . . . Ugh? Heil Who???

Nasos, not Nazis, was the original abbreviation for the National Socialist German Workers' Party. However, German writer Konrad Heiden, who had little use for them, bastardized Nasos into Nazis as a means of poking fun at them. Nazi is derived from a Bavarian word that means "simple-minded."

Gentlemen Don't Do That Sort of Thing

Early in the war Lieutenant General Sir Frank Mason-MacFarlane, a British officer who had served as military attaché in Berlin prior to hostilities, suggested using a high-powered telescopic rifle to assassinate Adolf Hitler. The idea was rejected as being "unsportsmanlike." Later, however, the assassination of General Erwin Rommel was supposed to be one of four covert actions as a prelude for Operation Crusader, the British counteroffensive against the Germans in North Africa. Six officers and 53 commandos came ashore from the submarines *Torbay* and *Talisman.* None of the actions were successful.

If at First You Don't Succeed . . .

Anti-Hitler German officers tried and failed twice to kill the Nazi leader during one week in March 1943. In the second attempt Colonel Rudolph von Gertsdorff had to flush the fuse of a bomb down a toilet when Hitler left a meeting before the bomb could be detonated. The incident took place at the Zeughaus exhibition hall in Berlin. The conspirators, most of whom were by this time nearing mental breakdowns, decided to compose themselves before trying again. It would be more than a year before another attempt was made.

If at First You Don't Succeed, Part II

Wernher von Braun, the German rocket expert who contributed to the development of the V-2 during the war and afterward put his talents to work for NASA and the American space program, failed mathematics and physics while attending school in France.

Special Delivery for the Führer

The Royal Air Force marked the anniversary of Adolf Hitler's 10th year in power by conducting its first daylight raid on Berlin. The attack took place while the official ceremonies were under way.

Follow the Leader, Nazi Style

It is commonly known that besides Hitler and Eva Braun, Josef and Magda Goebbels also committed suicide in the Führer Bunker (after poisoning their children). What isn't widely known is that no less than three other Nazis joined them in the pact of death: Chief of Staff General Hans Krebs; Hitler's adjutant, General Wilhelm Burgdorf; and Captain Franz Schedle, commander of the SS bunker guards all committed suicide also.

Jeez . . . Can't They Take a Joke?

When Adolf Hitler was told that France and Britain had declared war on Germany as a result of the invasion of Poland, the Führer slumped in his chair and was silent for a few moments. Then, looking up at the generals around him, he asked, "Well . . . what do we do now?"

There's One in Every Group

The two infamous slapping incidents that almost cost General George S. Patton his command were known to several correspondents who chose not to report or file anything about them. The story broke when syndicated columnist Drew Pearson decided it was a scoop he couldn't resist.

The Normandy beach antilanding obstacles were the brainchild of Rommel. Some poles had mines affixed to their tops, whereas others were designed to rip holes in Allied landing craft.
—*U.S. Air Force photo*

The gnarled, rotting remains of a few poles, silent sentinels to the 1944 invasion, can still be seen at Normandy during low tide.
—Photo by author

In what has become a legend within a legend, U.S. 82nd Airborne Division Private John Steele had the misfortune of having his parachute get caught on the church steeple in Ste.-Mère-Église on D-Day. Several other troopers and local residents remember the grim sight of Steele hanging limp in his harness as the battle raged around him. It wasn't until later that they discovered he was playing dead.
—Photo by author

"Steeple Jack" Steele Ste.-Mère-Église

When the 82nd Airborne Division "dropped in" on the French village of Ste.-Mère-Église in the vanguard of the D-Day assault shortly after midnight on June 6, 1944, there was an unexpected reception committee waiting for them in the church square. Shortly before the drop began, a house near the church had caught fire. Consequently the entire area around the church was full of people passing buckets of water and German troops observing the goings-on. At least two troopers landed in the burning house. Paratrooper John Steele was somewhat more fortunate, his chute getting caught on the church steeple. Steele, who was shot in the foot, dropped his knife trying to cut himself free. When he realized he was helpless with scores of Germans below him firing skyward, Steele simply played dead. Two hours later he was cut down and taken prisoner by the Germans.

Long Before He Ever Heard About Thrifts . . .

Alan Cranston, the future U.S. Senator from California, was sued by Adolf Hitler for copyright infringement of *Mein Kampf.* Cranston, a news correspondent in Europe in the 1930s, had read both the original in German and the U.S. version. After deciding too much had been edited out in the translation, Cranston published *Adolf Hitler's Own Book.* The Cranston version sold a half-million copies before a U.S. injunction forced him to discontinue offering it.

Ahhh . . . Not Right Now, But Thanks for Thinking of Us

The U.S. was actually invited to join Japan, Germany, and Italy as a member of the Tripartite Pact alliance on October 13, 1940. The offer to the U.S. was extended by Japan, who said America would be welcome as a member "in the spirit of the new order . . . in which . . . the natural geographic divisions of the earth established in complementary fashion" would be the goal.

Pick a Card, Any Card . . .

British magician Jasper Maskelyne commanded several fellow magicians in a unit commonly called the Magic Gang. Operating in North Africa until shortly after the Battle of El Alamein, they used tricks and the art of illusion to baffle the Germans in the desert. Among their more interesting achievements were hiding the Suez Canal, moving Alexandria Harbor, turning tanks into trucks, creating entire armies out of shadows, launching a phantom fleet of submarines, and materializing a battleship. He and his men were so successful the Gestapo added Maskelyne to its infamous Black List and placed a sizable bounty on him.

Just a Little Something for a Rainy Day

Martin Bormann, who was sentenced to death in absentia by the Nuremberg war crimes trials and whose whereabouts remain a mystery to this day, began a program of transporting gold, jewels, and art treasures out of occupied Europe by U-boat to destinations in South America. Starting as early as 1943 and continuing right up through April 1945, Bormann is believed to have diverted several hundred million dollars to Argentina alone, where it was used to provide sanctuary for numerous Nazis who vanished around the time Bormann did.

Big Tank Crushing Little Car . . . Take 147

The Soviets were quite serious about recording the war for posterity. One effort, on June 13, 1943, involved continuous filming for 24 hours. It involved nearly 250 cameramen recording the conflict from 140 vantage points. The finished product was an eight-reel film titled, appropriately, *Day of War.* It packed movie houses in the USSR, the U.S., and Britain whenever it was shown. In all, more than 100 Soviet combat photographers lost their lives in combat situations during the war.

The Café John Steele, around the corner from the church and its expansive square in Ste.-Mère-Église, commemorates the legend of the paratrooper everyone who was there on the morning of June 6, 1944 remembers.

—Photo by author

Finzie, Time Out—We Can't Play Yet

Because Canada was expecting large shipments of war matériel from the U.S. in September 1939, Canada waited until seven days after Britain, Australia, New Zealand, and India declared war on Germany before it did likewise. The U.S., which was operating under the laws of neutrality, would have been obliged not to send the shipments on to Canada had it joined the other countries in the Dominion in declaring war immediately after the invasion of Poland on September 1. Canada's delay permitted the delivery from the U.S.

Oh, That's Smart, Real Smart

The U.S. was the only major power that did not have an organized intelligence operation at the outbreak of war in Europe in 1939.

Not Exactly an Overwhelming Mandate

The U.S. Selective Service Act, which had been law for one year in 1940, was continued in 1941 by a margin of one vote in the House of Representatives, less than four months before the attack on Pearl Harbor.

Seeing Is Believing, or Is It?

During the war there were several instances in which U.S. pilots in the European theater of operations reported sighting disk-shaped flying objects that they didn't recognize as any known aircraft, Allied or Axis. Among airmen these UFOs quickly became known as Foo Fighters. As the instances increased, any pilot reporting such sightings was almost certain to be removed from flight duty. However, on June 24, 1947, more than two years after the war in Europe had ended, a Boise, Idaho, businessman named Kenneth Arnold encountered Foo Fighters while piloting a private plane near Mt. Rainier, Wash. He described the unidentified flying objects he saw as resembling "pie plates skipping over the water." Newspaper reporters picked up the story and coined the term flying saucers.

No Goose Stepping in the Dance Scenes, Please

The first recipient of an Academy Award (Oscar) for Best Actor, Emil Jannings in 1928, later made propaganda films for Germany during the war. Jannings had won the award for his work in *The Last Command* and *The Way of All Flesh*. The first Hollywood actor drafted into the U.S. Army was Sterling Holloway.

It Really Was a Wonderful Life

Actor Jimmy Stewart, who enlisted and flew 20 missions over Germany during the war, came home a colonel and reached the postwar rank of general in the Air Force Reserve. It is the highest rank attained by any member of the entertainment field who served in the war.

Frankly, Reichsmarschall, I Don't Give a Damn

Because he thought it would have considerable propaganda value, Hermann Goering offered what amounted to a $5,000 reward for the capture of a certain American Army Air Force officer, tail gunner Clark Gable.

"I See Nothing, Colonel Hogan, Nothing!"

Actor John Banner, who is best remembered for his portrayal of the light-witted Sergeant Schultz in the television series *Hogan's Heroes,* was a Jew who left Austria after the Nazis took over the country in 1938. During the war years Banner posed for U.S. recruiting posters.

The Real Story About the Iwo Jima Flag

The campaign for Iwo Jima began on February 19 and lasted for 26 days. The first flag raised on Mt. Suribachi, on February 23, 1945, was by Marines H. O. Hansen, E. I. Thomas, H. B. Shrier, J. R. Michaels, and C. W. Lindberg. It is recorded in U.S. Navy photo 304841. It was a relatively small flag one of the previously mentioned Marines had brought with him and lashed to an iron pipe. It is not the raising seen in the Pulitzer-Prize-winning photo by Associated Press photographer Joe Rosenthal. That one was a much larger ensign that came from LST-779 down on the beach. However, Rosenthal's photo was so dramatic and so captured the indomitable spirit of not only the Marines but American fighting men in all theaters of the war that it became one of the three most famous photos of World War II. The other two are the sinking of the battleship USS Arizona (BB-39), on the cover of this book, and the "Jaws of Death" Normandy landing photo on page 2.

—National Archives photos

The first Soviet flag was raised in Berlin over the Reichstag building on April 13, 1945, while the battle for the city was still going on.
—Courtesy of Sovfoto

Poetic Justice for Old Glory

The first American flag to fly over Berlin after Germany surrendered was the same flag that had flown over the U.S. Capitol in Washington, D.C., on December 8, 1941, the day the U.S. declared war on Japan.

Pssst! Want to See a French Flag?

The only location in Paris where the French flag, the Tricolor, was legally displayed during the German occupation was at Les Invalides, the army museum. It did not fly from a public building for four years until August 19, 1944, six days before the city's liberation, when members of the Resistance hoisted the flag at the Prefecture of Police building on the Île de la Cité across from Notre Dame.

Hooray for Hollywood

The only industry that provided its products free of charge to the U.S. government for use by military personnel was the film industry. Hollywood made more than 43,000 prints of virtually all its feature films available for the entertainment of servicemen.

Ah, Shucks

The American singer voted the most popular by troops during the war was not Frank Sinatra, not Bing Crosby, not Kate Smith. It was country-western singer Roy Acuff.

Backing Up Their Votes for War with Action

The first member of the House of Representatives to enlist after war was declared against Japan was Representative Lyndon Baines Johnson of Texas. He received a Navy commission as a lieutenant commander and saw limited action in the Pacific before President Roosevelt recalled all members of Congress. Senator Henry Cabot Lodge II of Massachusetts was the first member of the Senate to enlist. He served in North Africa. Nineteen years later Johnson and Lodge each found themselves second to others when they ran as the Democratic and Republican vice-presidential candidates with John F. Kennedy and Richard M. Nixon, respectively.

You Should See This Guy Toss a Grenade!

The only major league baseball player to serve in both world wars was Hank Gowdy, who had been a member of the New York Giants and Boston Braves between 1910 and 1930.

The first baseball player drafted in the war was Hank Greenberg of the Detroit Tigers.

Pilots Wanted: No Experience Necessary

The Allied air forces managed to overpower the German Luftwaffe not because heavy bombing had reduced the Reich's capacity to produce aircraft but because of a shortage of qualified German pilots. Overall armament production in Germany remained high until February 1944.

American Ingenuity, It Works Every Time

While considering the low-level bombing that would be required during the Doolittle Raid on Tokyo, it was discovered that the regular bombsights on the B-25s would be ineffective. Captain C. R. Greening, a pilot in the 17th Bombardment Group (which flew the mission), created a device that made the bombsight work perfectly. The cost for the added material was 15 cents per bombsight.

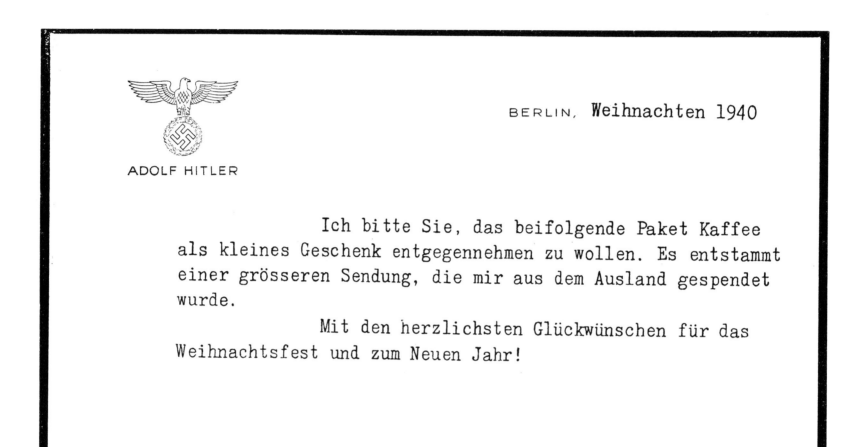

BERLIN, Weihnachten 1940

ADOLF HITLER

Ich bitte Sie, das beifolgende Paket Kaffee als kleines Geschenk entgegennehmen zu wollen. Es entstammt einer grösseren Sendung, die mir aus dem Ausland gespendet wurde.

Mit den herzlichsten Glückwünschen für das Weihnachtsfest und zum Neuen Jahr!

Hitler's June 1941 attack on the Soviet Union (Operation Barbarossa) was something he was fully committed to until December 1940, six months earlier. Yet conquering the Soviet Union wasn't the only thing the German Führer had on his mind that December, as his seasonal "Christmas" cards show. Packets of coffee, in short supply because of rationing, were included to recipients of his holiday cheer.

—Author's collection

Astrologically Speaking, Führer, Stay in Bed

Adolf Hitler had two horoscopes that predicted the outbreak of war in 1939, victories until 1941, difficulty in April 1945, and peace in August. The first was from November 9, 1918, and the second was done on the day he took power, January 30, 1933. Both horoscopes also noted that Germany would begin to rise again in 1948.

Perhaps He Was Psychic

In May and early June 1944 the *London Daily Telegraph* found itself at the center of one of the most intriguing coincidences of the war. Several answers it had published for its popular crossword puzzle turned out to be secret code names designated for the Normandy invasion, including *Overlord*, the name for the entire operation; *Utah* and *Omaha*, the two American beaches; *Mulberry*, the artificial harbors to be used; and *Neptune*, the name of the sea portion of Operation Overlord. There were also others of less significance, but these five particularly raised eyebrows at Supreme Headquarters Allied Expeditionary Force (SHAEF) command. After a thorough investigation by the military and Scotland Yard, the *Telegraph* and Leonard Sidney Dawe, its crossword puzzle compiler for more than 20 years, were found blameless of any intent to disclose classified information. The odds against such an extraordinary coincidence were later calculated to be several hundred thousand to one. (NOTE: *The Allies used more than 10,000 code names for various people, places, and operations during the war.*)

All the News We Like, We Print

There were 4,500 newspapers in Germany when the Nazis rose to power in 1933. By the eve of war in 1939 the number had dwindled to approximately 1,000, and they were controlled by or in sympathy with the Nazis.

And for You Sailors, We Have Rubber Duckies

The only Allied airborne troops that were considered expendable during the D-Day invasion were hundreds of rubber "paratrooper" dolls. Replete with firecrackers attached to them, they were dropped behind enemy lines in an effort to confuse the Germans.

Allied Bathroom Humor?

One of the most unusual uses of camouflage to hide the appearance of a weapon was the coloring and texture given to a plastic explosive that the Allies placed on roads as a vehicle land mine. The innocuous but lethal ordinance was made to resemble cow manure.

Nothing Personal, Ma'am, It Was My Job

Some years after the war, Italian journalist Oriana Fallaci was in Florida interviewing World War II veteran Donald K. Slayton. During their exchange Fallaci discovered the man she was talking to had taken part in the October 1943 air raid of Florence, Italy, which had destroyed her home. Slayton, better known as "Deke" rather than Donald, was one of the Original Seven Project Mercury astronauts.

Handicapped? Who's Handicapped?

Douglas Bader left the Royal Air Force after losing both legs in a car crash in 1931. He rejoined in 1939 and became a fighter ace during the Battle of Britain, scoring 23 kills.

But How Fast Could It Corner?

Porsche, famous throughout the world for its expensive, fast cars, designed and built the dreaded Tiger Tanks for Germany.

The insurrection that broke out in Paris as the Allies drew near began at the Prefecture of Police building (not visible in photo) directly across from Notre Dame Cathedral and quickly spilled into the surrounding streets and finally the whole city. If you look carefully in the clearing of smoke, a bicycle wheel is visible in this August 1944 photo.

—Presse-Liberation photo

Same corner, but a more passive scene four decades later. Coincidentally a moped appeared on the scene in time to make the comparison complete.

—Photo by author

The Supreme Allied Commander, sans corncob pipe but with equally famous crunched cap, in Australia while awaiting his return to the Philippines.

—*U.S. Army photo*

Relatively Speaking

U.S. General Douglas MacArthur was an eighth cousin of British Prime Minister Winston Churchill and a sixth cousin of U.S. President Franklin D. Roosevelt. All three wartime leaders had a common ancestor, Sarah Barney Belcher of Taunton, Mass. As remarkable as the MacArthur-Churchill-Roosevelt relationship was, consider this: At the outbreak of World War I, three of the most powerful European thrones were occupied by *first* cousins: George V of England, Wilhelm II of Germany, and Nicholas II of Russia. They had all called Queen Victoria grandmother.

Sorry, Your Highness

After the Japanese attack on Pearl Harbor, the city of Mikado, Michigan, officially changed its name to MacArthur, Michigan.

Doug, Did It Ever Occur to You . . .

General Douglas MacArthur had been notified of the attack on Pearl Harbor nearly eight hours before his command in the Philippines was attacked. Yet as had been the case at Oahu, MacArthur's planes remained on the ground and were relatively easy targets. Admiral Husband E. Kimmel and General Walter C. Short were both fired for their unpreparedness in Hawaii. General MacArthur was not.

Go Two Lights, Make a Left, Look for a Church . . .

In order to locate their objective during the liberation of Paris in August 1944, the 2nd Battalion, 12th Regiment, of the U.S. Army's 4th Division used a tourist guide map that one of its officers traded two packs of cigarettes for. Without the map they couldn't find the Prefecture of Police building, which is directly across from Notre Dame Cathedral.

Not the Kind of Stuff a Proper Chap Would Do

The British organization with the innocuous-sounding name London Controlling Section (LCS) was anything but mundane. Created by Prime Minister Winston Churchill, its function was to deceive the Germans about plans and operations through the use of misleading acts, strategems, lies, deceits, plots and counterplots, stealth, and treachery. Among its more bizarre operations was the episode that was the basis for the book and movie *The Man Who Never Was.* It involved creating a believable background for a fictitious officer whose body would be "washed" ashore on the Spanish coast in the hope that the Axis would think it was a dead secret courier. The body, with an attaché case handcuffed to it, carried papers identifying it as a Major Martin. The case contained "secret" plans calling Greece and Sardinia the primary choices for an Allied invasion (while Sicily was the real target). The Germans believed the ploy, but the Italians were not convinced.

What Are You Going to Do When You Grow Up?

Claus von Bulow, the Rhode Island financier who was the subject of the book and movie *Reversal of Fortunes,* had been a page at the wedding of Reichsmarschall Hermann Goering in the 1930s. On March 16, 1982, von Bulow was convicted of twice trying to kill his heiress wife with insulin injections so that he could collect a $14 million inheritance and marry his mistress.

Top Veteran in Congress

The most decorated World War II veteran ever elected to Congress was U.S. Senator Daniel Ken Inouye (D-Hawaii). Inouye, a third-generation American of Japanese ancestry, was awarded the Distinguished Service Medal, Bronze Star, Purple Heart with clusters, and five battle stars.

General Douglas MacArthur's sixth and fifth cousins, Prime Minister Winston Churchill and President Franklin D. Roosevelt, at the Yalta Conference in February 1945. Their get-together was for matters something more serious than would be discussed at a family reunion.
—British Information Services photo

Never Have So Many . . . Heard an Imposter

Winston Churchill's stirring "We shall fight on the beaches" speech heard on the BBC on June 4, 1940, in England and around the world was actually made by 37-year-old actor Norman Shelley of the BBC repertory company. Churchill had made the speech in Parliament, but when the BBC asked him to repeat it on the air he declined, pointing out that he was preoccupied with the evacuation of Dunkirk. Churchill himself suggested they find someone who might sound like him. In a London *Daily Mail* interview in 1979, Shelley told the paper how his selection came about: "I was a fan of Winnie. I had imitated his voice around the BBC. Someone must have remembered this, because they summoned me to the old transcription Service Studios near Regent's Park, gave me a copy of his speech, sat me down, and told me to get on with it. It was just another job. As I recall I did it in a couple of takes." After hearing Shelley's reading, Churchill agreed to let the actor do it. "Very nice. He's even got my teeth right," the PM commented. The imitation was good enough to fool Churchill's closest friends. It was reportedly the only time Churchill permitted such an act.

Not Now, Fellas, We're Kind of Busy

In what had to be a confusing and humiliating response, the U.S. refused to accept the declarations of war presented to it by Slovakia on December 12 and Croat on December 14, 1941.

A Rose by Any Other Name

Did you ever wonder how the "Axis" got its name? When Mussolini returned to Italy to report on his October 1936 meeting with Hitler, he addressed a gathering in Milan. He didn't tell them he and the German Führer had made a secret alliance whereby the foreign policies of the two countries would work in concert with each other. But he did coin the name they, and later their Japanese partners and others, would become infamously known by when he told his audience: "This vertical line between Rome and Berlin is not a partition but rather an axis round which all European states animated by the will to collaboration and peace can also collaborate." It wasn't the first time the *Duce* had considered the term. In 1923 he had penned a letter that included the notation "the axis of European history" goes to Berlin.

Flexing U.S. Naval Muscle in Tokyo Bay

The U.S. Navy gathered what is considered by many to have been the greatest exhibition of naval strength in history for the Japanese surrender ceremonies in Tokyo Bay in September 1945. The massive armada that made its way to the waters of the Japanese capital included 23 aircraft carriers, 12 battleships, 26 cruisers, and 313 destroyers and other ships for a grand total of 374 vessels. Never before or since has a vanquished enemy had the opportunity to see so dramatically so great a portion of a victor's might at its doorstep.

They Were Still a Force to Contend With

When Japan surrendered to the Allies in 1945, it still had more than 2 million combat-ready troops and 9,000 aircraft to protect the home islands. The Imperial Japanese Navy, however, had been all but eliminated.

Yo, Frankie, Check Out the New Plane

The German aircraft producer Messerschmitt had designed, but not built, two long-range bombers that he named after the city that was their intended target: New York.

Despite the German surrender of Paris and the entry of the Allies on August 26, 1944, snipers broke up the festivities in the Place de la Concorde more than once on Liberation Day. In response to a warning from his commander to "watch out for the Fifth Column," a gunner in the tank "Filibuster" blasted that specific Corinthian column along the facade of the Hotel Crillon (see banner on the building on the left). The warning, however, had been a reference to collaborationist snipers, not the architecture.
—USIS photo

The Hotel Crillon as it appears today. Notice the difference in color of the replacement fifth column from the originals.
—Photo by author

A pleasant-looking French farmhouse less than a mile behind Utah Beach and its still formidable-looking former German neighbor.
                                                        —Photo by author

Oh, So That's What Snafu Means

In a classic case of mistaken identity, shipments of wartime matériel destined for Milne Bay, New Guinea, wound up being sent to Fall River, Mass., where they remained unaccounted for a considerable time. But there was an explanation, sort of. The code name for Milne Bay was Fall River.

Harry Who, Soldier?

During the Battle of the Bulge, General Omar Bradley was challenged by American troops on the lookout for Germans dressed in U.S. uniforms. He was asked to name the capital of Illinois and correctly responded "Springfield." Next question was where is the scrimmage position of a guard in football, to which the general snapped, "Between the center and tackle." However, on three separate challenges he failed to identify the husband of pinup girl and movie star Betty Grable. Nonetheless, Bradley was permitted to pass, and from that time on would remember who bandleader Harry James was.

Ah, C'mon, Mate, Do I Look Like a Jerry?

British commandos who crossed the English Channel and attacked Germans in France the day the German-French armistice was signed were almost prevented from landing back in England. One boatload of commandos was delayed at gunpoint at Folkestone harbor for several hours because they carried no identification.

The Allied Solution Was to Bomb Them All

In an effort to thwart Allied bombing raids on certain German cities, reproductions of Berlin, Hamburg, and other areas were built near enough to the actual sites to confuse aircraft. However, they were far enough away to provide safety for the inhabitants. There were no less than five copies of Berlin alone sprinkled across the German landscape in giant scale.

Tanks, but No Tanks

During the Battle of Britain, Prime Minister Winston Churchill sent the last 70 tanks on the island to the British forces fighting in North Africa. He felt that if the situation in Great Britain got to a point where the last 70 tanks would be a crucial ingredient, the battle would already be lost. In justifying their movement to Egypt, Churchill told Parliament: "I have not become the King's First Minister to preside over the liquidation of the British Empire."

Not Bad for a West Point Dropout

U.S. Army General Courtney Hicks Hodges was forced to leave the U.S. Military Academy at West Point in 1906 because he failed geometry. Hodges immediately enlisted in the Army and became a private. He was commissioned a second lieutenant in 1909, one year behind his former classmates. While under his command in World War II the U.S. First Army liberated Paris, defeated the Germans in the Ardennes, made the first Rhine crossing at Remagen, and met the Soviets on the Elbe.

Nature Was the Greater Enemy

The greatest damage to the U.S. Navy in the Pacific theater was caused by a typhoon, not the Japanese. On December 17–18, 1944, a typhoon approximately 500 miles off the east coast of the Philippines took a toll that included 769 lives, damage to eight aircraft carriers, the capsizing of three destroyers, 150 planes washed off the decks of carriers, and damage to a number of other ships.

The most expensive bottle of Coca-Cola ever sold, according to the German Ministry of Propaganda in World War II, went for a whopping $10,000 in January 1944. The Josef Goebbels exaggeration specialists reported that supplies were so short for U.S. troops in Italy that 10 grand was the going rate for the soft drink. The GIs in this photo do not seem to have a limited supply.

—Courtesy of The Coca-Cola Company

The Nazi report about supplies was wrong, to say the least—two bottles of Coke were *auctioned*, not sold, and the price was inflated. Here's the true story, according to *Washington Post* columnist Joseph Mastrangelo, who found the reference among dispatches sent back by the late Ernie Pyle. A GI serving in Italy received two bottles of Coke in the mail from a buddy back home. It was the first time the soldier or any of his companions had seen a Coke in nearly a year. He drank one and decided to raffle off the other and use the proceeds to help children whose fathers had died in battle. The raffle tickets sold for a quarter each, and in no time the pot had grown to just over $1,000. Then another GI contributed a miniature bottle of Coke that he had received from home. The addition of a second bottle, albeit small, pumped a second life into the drawing. One officer, Colonel James R. Couch of Alexandria, Va., bought 40 tickets alone. By New Year's Day 1944 the amount collected had reached $4,000, and the drawing was held. The numbered slips went into an artillery shell casing and the brigade commander drew out two slips. Everybody wanted the regular-size bottle, and the miniature was jokingly referred to as the "booby prize." The regular-size bottle of Coke was won by Hackensack, N.J., resident Sergeant William DeSchneider, 13th Field Artillery Brigade. Sergeant Lawrence Presnell, First Field Artillery Observation Batallion, Ft. Bragg, N.C., a native of Fayetteville, N.C., won the miniature. Presnell's little Coke bottle remained intact until it was accidentally broken by one of his children. Efforts to locate DeSchneider and find out what happened to the most expensive Coca-Cola bottle in the world have been unsuccessful.

Beats the Heck Out of Sending Smoke Signals

To confuse Japanese who were listening to U.S. Marine Corps radio transmissions in the Pacific during the war, the Marines took full advantage of the more than 300 Navajo-speaking American Indians in the Corps by employing them as radio code talkers.

No Thanks, We Already Have a "Little Italy"

The only known incident in the war in which a captured or liberated people expressed a strong interest in becoming the 49th state in the U.S. came about during the occupation of Sicily. U.S. military officials there reported back to Washington that the inquiries were indeed serious. By 1947 the effort had come to the point that a Sicilian bandit named Salvatore Giuliano wrote to President Harry S Truman and asked for help in liberating Sicily. The movement attracted many nationalists who resented Rome's treatment and also sought protection from what they considered a communist takeover of Italy. The separatist cause became a thing of the past by the 1950s as various leaders were unable to unify and settle differences among themselves.

Did You Guys Ever Hear About "the War Effort"?

The only American labor union to violate the AFL and CIO pledge not to strike during the war was the United Mine Workers, who under John L. Lewis walked off their jobs four times.

How the Jeep Got Its Name

In the 1930s a vehicle that bore a strong resemblance to the Jeep appeared in *Popeye the Sailor* cartoons. The sound it made when animated was "Jeep, Jeep". In 1940 the U.S. Army introduced the vehicle it was putting into service as: "A quarter-ton GP truck," GP meaning general purpose. It looked a lot like Popeye's little car. Less than a year later the DeVilbiss Co., of Toledo ran an ad in *Time* magazine showing the same vehicle and identified it as a "Peep." According to the copy, Peeps were reconnaissance cars used by the 1st Armored Division. However, the vehicle was almost universally called a Jeep, perhaps by the Popeye influence, perhaps by the phonetic sound when pronouncing the initials GP.

The aircraft produced more than any other by the U.S. in the war was the B-24 Liberator, of which 18,188 were made. Liberators were flown by the Army, Navy, RAF, and other Allies. In this photo the 7th Air Force's famous Kansas Cyclone drops 500-pound bombs on the Japanese stronghold of Truk. The Great Barrier Reef, which made the atoll a moated fortress, can be clearly seen at the bottom of the photo.
—U.S. Air Force photo

The notion that Adolf Hitler's warped mind concocted the idea to blow up the 20 beautiful Paris bridges that cross the Seine is incorrect. The bridges had been deliberately prepared for just such an eventuality by the French themselves more than 70 years earlier. The French had passed laws that provided for the installation of special metal pans under every bridge in France so that they could destroy them in a war emergency. The Germans found the pans intact in 1944. The photo is of Pont Alexander III, considered to be the most beautiful of the bridges in Paris.

—*French Tourist Office photo*

The only conscientious objector to become a Medal of Honor
recipient during World War II was U.S. Army Pfc. Desmond T. Doss
of Lynchburg, Va., who, as a member of the medical corps., is
credited with personally saving the lives of 75 wounded soldiers,
while himself under heavy enemy fire, who were trapped on a
50-foot ridge, Maeda Escarpment, on the southern end of Okinawa.
The medal was presented by President Harry S Truman during
ceremonies at the White House on October 12, 1945. Doss, who also
saw action on Guam and Leyte, also received the Bronze Star with
cluster for valor and the Purple Heart with two oak leaves. Drafted
in 1942 and classified as a conscientious objector, the then
26-year-old Doss was a member of the 307th Infantry Medical
Detachment, 1st Battalion, of the 77th Infantry, the "Statue of
Liberty" Division.

—Courtesy of Betty Cooner

"A Few Good Men" . . . Sometimes They're Short

According to an article in the *Des Moines Register* in early 1942, on his third attempt to enlist, Albert (Jack) Brown, 17, of Iowa City, Iowa, became the shortest member of the U.S. Marine Corps in World War II by working hard to meet the Corps minimum 64-inch requirement. Initially Brown was measured a quarter of an inch below the minimum. Not dismayed, the future leatherneck went to the State University of Iowa's fieldhouse and hung by his knees from parallel bars and did other stretching exercises for a week before returning to the enlistment center. Some improvement, but still too short was the verdict. After another week of exercise Brown returned to be measured for the third, and final time, and made it. At full stretch the 141-pound Brown, a two year varsity football player in high school, towered to 5'4" on the nose.

Come Out, Come Out, Wherever You Are . . .

The U.S. 2nd Armored Division employed a tank equipped with a loudspeaker to get German villages and towns to surrender. Lieutenant Arthur T. Hadley, a psychological warfare specialist, was commander of the tank. The messages Hadley and his crew broadcast told the civilian population they had nothing to fear from the Americans and pointed out how badly the war was going for Germany.

Too Much Yank Yackity-yak

After the war it was learned that U.S. pilots shot down the plane carrying Japanese admiral Yamamoto with the help of Ultra intelligence. The British charged that the U.S. compromised the security of the code breaking, but the U.S. denied the charges and defended its position. Previously secret wartime messages released to the U.S. National Archives in 1981 substantiate the British charges. American fighter pilots talked over the air so much about the Yamamoto incident that the Japanese suspected their codes were being read and immediately changed them. It took four months for the U.S. to crack the new code.

Join the Navy . . . and See the White House

The five men who followed U.S. Army General Dwight D. Eisenhower to the Oval Office were all U.S. Navy veterans. In order: John F. Kennedy, Lyndon B. Johnson, Richard M. Nixon, Gerald R. Ford, and Jimmy Carter. Though not a WWII veteran, Carter is the only U.S. Naval Academy graduate in the group. Ford, who was assistant navigation officer on the USS *Monterey*, was also the director of physical education aboard the aircraft carrier when not in the plotting room.

Join the Navy . . . and Make Influential Friends

John Mitchell, the future Nixon administration attorney general, was Lieutenant John F. Kennedy's commanding officer in the Solomon Islands. The intelligence officer for the flotilla that *PT-109* was assigned to (and who coauthored the official report on the loss of the boat) was Lieutenant Byron R. White, future justice of the U.S. Supreme Court. *PT-109* was cut in half by the Japanese destroyer *Amagiri* on the night of August 1–2, 1943.

Postscript to the Bridge on the River Kwai

On September 11, 1944, U.S. submarines sank two Japanese transport ships that had more than 2,218 U.S., British, and Australian prisoners of war on board. These troops were survivors of the building of the infamous bridge on the River Kwai. Nearly 1,300 of the POWs were killed when the *Rakuyo Maru* and the *Kachidoki Maru* sank within minutes. The U.S. submarines rescued 159, and Japanese ships picked up another 792 and reimprisoned them. Only 606 of the original 2,218 survived the war.

General Douglas MacArthur knew a good slogan or quote when he uttered one and played to the hilt his famous "I shall return" pledge to the Philippines. MacArthur ordered cigarette and candy bar wrappers imprinted with the initials I.S.R. sent to the islands by submarines during the Japanese occupation. The general is seen here addressing Filipino volunteers at Banambang on January 20, 1945, after making good on his promise.

—U.S. Army photo

Now Ian, About All These Notes You're Taking

The personal assistant to Admiral John Godfrey, director of naval intelligence in the British Admiralty during the war, was Lieutenant Commander Ian Fleming. After the war Fleming named his estate on the Caribbean island of Jamaica *Golden Eye*, the code name for Prime Minister Winston Churchill's plan to secure Gibraltar if Spain had joined the Axis. Fleming, of course, went on to create superspy James Bond in the successful book series.

Lucky Luciano's Air Force: We Deliver

Nazi propagandists took full advantage of the name a U.S. B-17 bomber crew had painted on their plane and flight jackets. When they were forced to bail out over Germany and were subsequently captured, the Nazis released stories that the U.S. Army Air Force had released dangerous Chicago gangsters from prison to bomb German cities. The name the crew had painted on the plane and their flight jackets was *Murder, Inc.*

Teamwork Paid Off

The U.S. Navy trained personnel from 14 different Allied countries at its Submarine Chaser Training Center in Miami, Fla., during 1942–43. It was the first time so large a number of foreign naval nationals participated in training usually reserved for U.S. Navy officers and ratings.

The Mysterious Ice Cream Ship: USS Double Dip?

Throughout the war U.S. troops in other branches of the service envied the legendary meals enjoyed by U.S. Navy personnel. However, many simply refused to believe that the Navy actually had a ship whose sole purpose was to make ice cream for sailors in the South Pacific. The ship was reportedly capable of producing more than 5,000 gallons of ice cream per hour. (NOTE: *The name of the "ice cream ship" is not widely known. Anyone out there able to help solve the mystery?*)

Jolly Good Show

In a remarkable display of precision bombing on October 31, 1944, RAF planes bombed the Gestapo headquarters at Aarhus, Denmark, without damaging two hospitals that were hardly 100 yards away.

The Basement Is Full, What About the Attic?

The bronze sculpture of the Iwo Jima flag raising was unveiled at Arlington National Cemetery in 1954, but no home for the 130-ton white plaster cast model of the U.S. Marine Corps War Memorial could be found. The model remained in sculptor Felix de Weldon's Warwick, R.I., studio from 1954 until de Weldon donated it to the Marine Military Academy in Harlingen, Tex., in October 1981. Valued at $3.5 million, the 108-piece model takes four months to assemble. It was delivered to the MMA by nine 18-wheel flatbed trucks. Dedication ceremonies for the assembled model were on February 19, 1982, the 37th anniversary of the assault on Iwo Jima.

Sir, Was a Church in the Target Area?

Boise City, Okla., holds the distinction of being the only mainland U.S. town bombed during the war. However, the incident was not the result of Axis ability to penetrate U.S. defenses. A U.S. Army Air Force bomber on a training mission from Dalhart, Tex., knocked out the local Baptist church and another building. The pilot had some serious explaining to do since the buildings he hit were more than 40 miles from his assigned targets. Fortunately there were no casualties in Boise City.

Germany lost 901 generals in and immediately after World War II, more than any other nation in any other war in history. In addition to combat deaths, accidents, and natural causes, an astonishing 101 German generals committed suicide, such as this Volkssturm (People's Army) general on the floor in the Leipzig city hall on April 19, 1945. German courts sentenced 25 SS and army generals to death for war crimes, and the Allied powers executed another 57 for the same reason.

—U.S. Army photo

The first Catholic mass in Normandy after the invasion was celebrated the morning of June 6 by Father Pierre Bin. The priest had been away from the region, but on learning about the invasion from friends in the Resistance, he pedaled his bike some 50 miles. "I had a pass from the Germans to permit me such movement, yet I was halted several times," he remembered in a 1984 interview with the author. "As I got nearer to my church the sounds of bombs grew louder." His church was undamaged. He recalled that the first American troops he met and invited to mass thanked him for the offer but reminded him they had something else to finish first that morning.

—Photo by author

After the war Oberstgruppenführer (General) Sepp Dietrich, commander of the 6th SS Panzer Division, and 73 of his troops were convicted of war crimes for the murder of American soldiers at Malmédy during the Ardennes offensive (the Battle of the Bulge). Though Dietrich was given a 25-year sentence, 43 of the defendants were sentenced to death. None were executed, however, due to the efforts and intervention of the American prosecutor. All had been released from prison by 1956.

—U.S. Army photo

Victors Are Never Tried for War Crimes

For a time during the Battle of Britain RAF pilots were ordered to destroy German air-sea rescue seaplanes (clearly marked with red crosses) to prevent rescued Luftwaffe pilots from fighting another day. The order met stiff resistance from most RAF pilots.

More Than Five Decades Later the Hunt Continues

The U.S. became the greatest haven for Nazi war criminals after the war, according to estimates of various organizations that continue to hunt such people. According to the German government, approximately 25,000 people were involved in the operation of the Nazi extermination camps. Only 10 percent of them have been brought to justice. The vast majority of war criminals passed themselves off as refugees at displaced persons camps and thereby gained freedom. In the first 36 years following the end of the war, the U.S. managed to deport only one accused Nazi. Current estimates suggest that 3,000 others are still alive and living in America.

Looks Like a Great Day to Have a Beer or Two

The only two civilian activities in Berlin that did not cease operations during the battle for the city were its 17 breweries and the weather bureau. Despite the chaos around them they performed without interruption through the surrender and occupation of Berlin as well.

Like, Hockey and Basketball Were Essential?

The only two professional sports that were prohibited during the war were automobile racing and horse racing. The first was for fuel consumption, the second was considered nonessential.

Coffee, Tea, or Politics?

On January 11, 1943, Franklin D. Roosevelt became the first U.S. President to fly in a plane when he boarded the *Dixie Clipper* in Miami on the first leg of the trip that would take him to the Casablanca conference. The pilot for the historic flight was Howard M. Cone, a Pan American employee and a lieutenant in the Naval Reserve.

Again, Jeanette? Again?

The only member of Congress to vote "no" when President Roosevelt asked for a declaration that "a state of war existed" between the U.S. and Japan was Representative Jeanette Rankin (R-Mont.). She had also voted no against the resolution for war with Germany in 1917.

Well, Hermie, It's Not Easy at the Top, Is It?

Reichsmarschall Hermann Goering personally destroyed Karinhall, his palatial estate, rather than let it fall into the hands of the advancing Soviets. Before leaving it for the last time on April 20, 1945, to attend a birthday celebration for Hitler, Goering pushed the plunger that blew it up. "Well, that's what you have to do sometimes when you're a crown prince," he told those around him. However, he waited until a convoy of no fewer than 24 trucks had departed with his antiques, furniture, paintings, and other valuables.

Rather Bad Show, Chaps, Don't You Agree?

Even though hostilities between Britain and Germany had been a fact shortly after the declaration of war that followed the Nazi invasion of Poland on September 1, 1939, Britain didn't confiscate or in any way restrict German-bound shipments leaving its ports until November 21.

Reichsführer-SS Heinrich Himmler, the chief of the SS, seen here in the early days of the group's rise, giving a stiff Nazi salute.
　　　　　　　　　　　　　　　　　　　　　　　　　—U.S. Army photo

WHAT EXACTLY WAS THE SS?

The Hollywood stereotype of the brutal SS guard smiling as he empties a gun into defenseless victims really doesn't go far enough to explain who, and what, the SS was. Besides being responsible for murdering millions of people, the SS was in actuality a rather complicated organization that managed to insert its influence and control in numerous activities of German life.

The Allgemeine-SS, with slightly more than 200 members, was the broad overall body. Though many in its ranks were card-carrying part-timers, the Allgemeine-SS was the tree that sprouted many branches of terror: the Waffen-SS (armed), the Gestapo, and the SS concentration and death camps. It also operated such diverse and profit-motivated businesses as mink ranches and herb gardens.

The first economic venture the SS became involved in was acquiring a small company that produced procelain products. The operation was quickly transferred to Dachau, where it turned out rather good porcelain figurines, vases, and so on, and a selection of official SS gift items. Carl Diebitsch, the designer of the SS uniforms and insignia, was the artistic director of the porcelain works.

In its 22-year history the Allgemeine-SS methodically became involved in every government ministry or medium-to-large-size company in Germany. If the SS didn't run the show, an SS member was most surely in a position of high authority. Some historians have compared the influence the SS wielded over Germany to the control the Jesuits have had in the Roman Catholic Church. In fact, Hitler himself once called SS chief Heinrich Himmler "my Ignatius Loyola" (the founder of the Jesuits).

When Hitler rose to power in Germany in January 1933, the SS was no more than a relatively small but elite personal bodyguard unit for the Führer. They were no match for the much larger and rowdy "Storm Troopers" of the SA (also known as the Brownshirts), which had been the military arm of the Nazi movement. In one of the great intrigues of prewar Nazism, Hitler managed to usurp the power of the Storm Troopers (who were loyal to the Nazi cause) with an ever-growing SS (who were personally loyal to Hitler himself).

The invasion of Poland had an effect on the balance of power between the paper pushers and political types in the Allgemeine-SS, who suddenly found themselves drafted into various branches of the German armed forces and the militaristic Waffen-SS. Ironically, a far greater number of Allgemeine-SS members served in the army, navy, and Luftwaffe than the Waffen-SS.

By the outbreak of war in 1939 the armed Waffen-SS had expanded to approximately 15,000 men. Before the German surrender in May 1945 it had become so large a force that it equaled the authority of the German army.

The once-touted pure Aryan composition of the Waffen-SS was only a myth by late 1944. Approximately 500,000 non-Germans filled the ranks of no less than 27 of the 40 Waffen-SS divisions. This meant that over half of the service's strength was from other areas of Europe. In addition, there were volunteer Americans and Asians who served, but the largest number of non-Germans was the nearly 100,000 Russians. Some other countries with large national representation in the Waffen-SS were Holland, 50,000; France, 20,000; Finland, 20,000; Norway, 6,000; and Denmark, 6,000.

Guess Who Pardoned Tokyo Rose?

Iva Ikuko Toguri d'Aquino was an American citizen who was visiting a sick relative in Japan when war broke out. A graduate of UCLA with a degree in zoology, she chose to work in the Japanese Broadcasting Company rather than be assigned to work in a factory. Although she insisted she was not Tokyo Rose, d'Aquino was convicted of treason and received a 10-year prison term and $10,000 fine. In January 1977 President Gerald R. Ford granted her a full pardon. The value of the sultry messages broadcast to U.S. troops in the Pacific by Tokyo Rose has always been questionable. Most servicemen claim to have enjoyed the music she played and found her remarks laughable. Iva d'Aquino is seen here in custody, shortly after the war ended, tending a garden in prison.

—Exclusive photo courtesy of George Schroth

...Briefly, and Without Comment

Karl Wojtyla, a Polish student who remained on Gestapo execution lists for years because he helped Jews escape, was ordained a priest in 1946. In 1978 he became Pope John Paul II.

★★★★★

Civilian deaths in the war were more than double those of military personnel. More than 38.5 million civilians of all nations died, whereas battle deaths accounted for slightly more than 14.9 million military personnel. In total, just under 53.5 million people were killed.

★★★★★

The first member of Parliament killed in the war was Ronald Cartland in 1940. He was the brother of romance novelist Barbara Cartland (who herself is related by marriage to Princess Diana).

★★★★★

The British used two different code names for their operation to employ a look-alike for Field Marshall Bernard Law Montgomery: Hambone and Copperhead. The individual selected was an actor, E. Clifton-James, who later wrote a book about his role and portrayed himself in the movie *I Was Monty's Double*. He had been recommended for the job by fellow actor Colonel David Niven. Unfortunately, the ruse had to be terminated when Clifton-James had difficulty living up to Montgomery's abhorrence for alcohol and tobacco. (Churchill's double, Alfred Chenfalls, was killed in the same plane crash that took the life of actor Leslie Howard.)

One of the most unusual devices for identification used by any nation in the war was the employing of fireworks by the U.S. during the North African invasion (Operation Torch). The Vichy French were expected to be hostile and resist any invasion attempt by the British, who had recently attacked the French fleet in the harbor. In an effort to convince the Vichy French at Oran that the invasion force was American and not British, the U.S. shot fireworks bombs that exploded high in the sky as 100-foot-wide displays of Old Glory. The U.S. troops also used loudspeakers that identified them as not being British troops.

★★★★★

The first public appearance, and first speech, General Charles de Gaulle made in France after the Normandy invasion was at Bayeux on June 14, 1944. His triumphant return to Paris in August 1944 was nearly his last public appearance, ever. From a vantage point in the Kriegsmarine headquarters on the Place de la Concorde, German navy Lieutenant Commander Harry Leithold watched the "Liberation Day" parade as it moved down the Champs Élysées. After lining up his submachine gun sights on a tall French officer in the center of the crowd below him, Leithold realized that the mob in the streets could easily seize and kill him if he opened fire. Leithold decided that the tall French officer wasn't worth it, no matter who he was. Later, while in a POW camp, Leithold saw a newspaper photo of de Gaulle and realized who he had almost shot.

★★★★★

The only American municipality to intentionally employ illiterates as sanitation men during the war was Oak Ridge, Tenn. It did so as part of national security. The U.S. government conducted atomic research projects at Oak Ridge. It was believed that if classified information escaped shredding and found its way into the garbage collection, illiterate sanitation employees would be unable to compromise security!

The first GI barbershop on the Normandy beaches was operated by Victor Lombardo approximately 1,000 feet from the shoreline on Utah Beach. In the photo Lombardo, who was with the quartermaster corps, tends to the needs of dental technician Sam Kravetz of the 1st Engineer Special Brigade.

—Courtesy of Murray D. Lombardo

★★★★★

The first land recaptured from the Germans in the war was Smolensk, Russia, by the Red Army in August 1941.

The first weather station to operate off an air strip in Europe after the Normandy invasion was Detachment Y, 21st Mobile Weather Squadron, in France.

★★★★★

The first Allied assistance for Tito's partisans came from the British in May 1943.

★★★★★

The first Italians to fight against the Germans after Italy broke with the Axis were the Italian Motorized Group (army).

The only U.S. army that had written orders mentioning Berlin as an objective was the Ninth Army, in a document titled "Letter of Instructions, #20." Commanding Lieutenant General William Simpson was aware that other armies in the Twelfth Army Group (First and Third) had received instructions that did not include the phrase "advance on Berlin." He believed his army had been selected to beat the Russians, and everybody else, there.

★★★★★

The only two Latin American nations that had combat troops in action during the war were Mexico and Brazil.

★★★★★

The largest Japanese spy ring was not in the U.S. but in Mexico, where it kept tabs on the U.S. Atlantic Fleet.

★★★★★

All 11 starting members of Montana State University's 1940–41 football team were killed in the war.

★★★★★

New Zealand, with under 3 million people, provided the highest proportion of its population for war service of any British dominion.

★★★★★

The only three countries that were represented by troops in all theaters of the war were the U.S., Great Britain, and New Zealand.

★★★★★

The first Soviet troops entered Berlin on April 22, 1945.

During what is known as the Battle of the Atlantic more than 2,600 ships (15 million tons) from both sides were sunk.

★★★★★

The first Jewish ghetto in Poland was established at Lodz in April 1940. On April 27 Heinrich Himmler ordered the creation of an extermination camp at Auschwitz, Poland. Of the 3.3 million Jews in Poland less than 10 percent would be alive by the time the killing at Auschwitz ended on October 30, 1944. In addition to Polish Jews, the camp was responsible for the deaths of Jews transported there from other occupied areas. The first victims executed at Auschwitz were Soviet POWs who were gassed on September 3, 1941.

★★★★★

The first country to mount organized resistance against German occupation was Yugoslavia, on December 3, 1941, under the leadership of General Draze Mihajlovic. He not only fought the Nazis but at times also fought the Communist partisans headed by Josef Broz, who was better known under his nom de guerre, Tito.

★★★★★

The first U.S. soldier to set foot on French soil in the war was Army Corporal Frank M. Koons, an American Ranger, in the Dieppe raid.

★★★★★

The first U.S. serviceman to land in Great Britain after the U.S. entered the war was Army Pfc. Melburn Hencke, who set foot on English soil on January 26, 1942.

The poster shown above was an effort by Germany in the early years of the war to recruit French workers by suggesting that helping the Nazis would save Europe from the Russians. When calls for volunteers fell short of manpower needs, the Third Reich pressed more than 7.5 million Europeans and 2 million POWs into forced labor.

—U.S. Army photo

★★★★★

APPENDICES

★★★★★

The 20 Largest Battleships in World War II

Ship and Country	Gross Tonnage	Length (feet)
Yamato, Japan	72,809*	862
Musashi, Japan	72,809†	862
Iowa, U.S. (BB-61)	55,710	887
New Jersey, U.S. (BB-62)	55,710	887
Missouri, U.S. (BB-63)	55,710	887
Wisconsin, U.S. (BB-64)	55,710	887
Bismarck, Germany	50,153	823
Tirpitz, Germany	50,153	823
Richelieu, France	47,500	812
Jean Bart, France	47,500	812
Hood, Great Britain	46,200	860
Washington, U.S. (BB-56)	44,800	729
North Carolina, U.S. (BB-55)	44,800	729
King George V, Great Britain	44,780	754
Prince of Wales, Great Britain	44,780	754
Duke of York, Great Britain	44,780	754
Anson, Great Britain	44,780	754
Howe, Great Britain	44,780	754
Nagato, Japan	42,785	725
Mutsu, Japan	42,785	725

*Although Yamato and Musashi were the same size, Yamato was the only battleship ever built to have 18-inch guns. Despite their size the guns were considerably less accurate than the 16-inch guns of the American Iowa class.
†It took 20 torpedo hits and 17 bombs to sink the Musashi during the Battle of Leyte Gulf.
‡The USS Tennessee (BB-43) and USS California (BB-44), at 40,500 tons and 624 feet long, would rank 21st and 22nd on the list.

Comparative American and German Officer Ranks

U.S. Army	Wehrmacht	SS
General of the Army* (5 stars)	Generalfeldmarschall	SS Reichsführer
General (4 stars)	Generaloberst	Oberstgruppenführer
Lieutenant general (3 stars)	General	Obergruppenführer
Major general (2 stars)	Generalleutnant	Gruppenführer
Brigadier general (1 star)	Generalmajor	Brigadeführer
—	—	Oberfuehrer
Colonel	Oberst	Standartenführer
Lieutenant colonel	Oberstleutnant	Obersturmbannführer
Major	Major	Sturmbannführer
Captain	Hauptmann	Hauptsturmführer
First lieutenant	Oberleutnant	Obersturmführer
Second lieutenant	Leutnant	Untersturmführer
Warrant officer	Unteroffizer	Hauptscharführer

*The only American to actually be designated a field marshall was General of the Army Douglas MacArthur. That title was bestowed by the Philippine, not the U.S., government. However, the five-star rank in the U.S. services is equal to field marshall.

Box Score
United States 6   Japan 4   Germany 2
Great Britain 6   France 2   Total = 20‡

The USS Arizona
and Other Battleships Not on the Above List of 20 Largest

The third American ship to carry the name USS *Arizona* (BB-39) was placed in commission in 1916 and to this day continues to appear on U.S. Navy lists as a member of the fleet in tribute to the men entombed aboard her. As a result, no other ship will ever carry the name. Of the approximately 1,550 Navy and Marine Corps personnel aboard *Arizona* on December 7, 1941, only 289 survived. Compared to the 42,000-plus ton giants listed in this section, the most famous U.S. battleship of all was small by comparison. When seaworthy, the *Arizona* had a normal displacement of 31,400 tons. At 608 feet long *Arizona,* and her sister ship USS *Pennsylvania* (BB-38), were the first American battleships to exceed 600 feet in length. A campaign to raise $500,000 for a memorial was begun in 1957 and included a benefit performance by entertainer Elvis Presley as well as support from the then popular television show "This Is Your Life" and from newspapers across the country. The memorial, dedicated on Memorial Day 1962, spans the *Arizona* itself, which was never raised from its watery grave.

★★★★★

Until the Japanese attack on Pearl Harbor, the navies of the world considered battleships the ultimate sea weapon, and the larger and heavier they were was supposed to suggest something about a country's sea power. Although Japan launched the two largest battleships ever built, aircraft carriers, not battleships, were the weapons Japan depended on for the initiation of hostilities with the U.S.

And it was aircraft carriers, American aircraft carriers, that turned the tide of war in the Pacific. It is interesting to note that while Japan's two Yamato-class battleships were by far the heaviest, the U.S. Iowa-class dreadnoughts were the longest.

★★★★★

Before World War II Germany had considered truly monster battleships (H class), which at 141,500 tons would have been nearly twice as large as Japan's *Yamato* and *Musashi.*

★★★★★

The USS *Nevada* (BB-36) and sister ship USS *Oklahoma* (BB-37) were the first battleships built to burn fuel oil.

★★★★★

The first post–World War I U.S. battleship to mount 16-inch guns was the USS *Maryland* (BB-46). Her sister ships, USS *Colorado* (BB-45) and USS *West Virginia* (BB-48), were likewise so armed. *West Virginia,* commissioned in 1923, was the newest U.S. battleship in the Pacific when World War II began.

The U.S. Battleship Fleet

With the exception of the historic trio from 1895, the list below includes only battleships that were part of the U.S. fleet when the war broke out or that were completed or planned while the war was in progress.

U.S. Battleships		Completed	Tonnage	Length	U.S. Battleships		Completed	Tonnage	Length
(no #)	USS *Maine*	1895			BB-48	USS *West Virginia*	1923	33,590	624
(no #)	*Texas*	1895			BB-55	USS *North Carolina*	1941	44,800	729
BB-1	USS *Indiana*	1895			BB-56	USS *Washington*	1941	44,800	729
BB-33	USS *Arkansas*	1912	26,100	562	BB-57	USS *South Dakota*	1941	42,000	680
BB-34	USS *New York*	1914	27,000	573	BB-58	USS *Indiana*	1942	42,000	680
BB-35	USS *Texas*	1914	27,000	573	BB-59	USS *Massachusetts*	1942	42,000	680
BB-36	USS *Nevada*	1916	29,000	583	BB-60	USS *Alabama*	1942	42,000	680
BB-37	USS *Oklahoma*	1915	29,000	583	BB-61	USS *Iowa*	1943	55,710	887
BB-38	USS *Pennsylvania*	1915	33,400	608	BB-62	USS *New Jersey*	1943	55,710	887
BB-39	USS *Arizona*	1916	33,400	608	BB-63	USS *Missouri*	1944	55,710	887
BB-40	USS *New Mexico*	1917	33,400	624	BB-64	USS *Wisconsin*	1944	55,710	887
BB-41	USS *Mississippi*	1917	33,000	624	BB-65	USS *Illinois*	Cancelled, 1945		
BB-42	USS *Idaho*	1919	33,000	624	BB-66	USS *Kentucky*	Cancelled, 1944		
BB-43	USS *Tennessee*	1919	40,500	624	BB-67	USS *Montana**	Cancelled, 1943		
BB-44	USS *California*	1919	40,500	624	BB-68	USS *Ohio*	Cancelled		
BB-45	USS *Colorado*	1921	33,590	624	BB-69	USS *Maine*	Cancelled		
BB-46	USS *Maryland*	1921	33,590	624	BB-70	USS *New Hampshire*	Cancelled		
BB-47	USS *Washington*	Cancelled			BB-71	USS *Louisiana*	Cancelled		

*Five Montana class ships (BB-67–71) were to have been 903 feet long and weighed 65,000 tons fully loaded.

The 20 Top Submarine Commanders of the U.S. Navy

As with fighter pilots, the U-boat commanders dominated their area of warfare. When this list had been compiled, it was interesting to note that the top U.S. submarine commander, Richard H. O'Kane, would place seventh in the top German 20 U-boat commanders based on the number of ships sunk. Gross tonnage was considered in the ranking only when two or more commanders sank an equal number of ships.

Commander/Submarine	Ships Sunk	Patrols
Richard H. O'Kane; *Tang*	31	5
Eugene B. Fluckey; *Barb*	25	5
Slade D. Cutter; *Seahorse*	21	4
Samuel D. Dealey; *Harder*	20.5	6
William S. Post, Jr.; *Gudgeon, Spot*	19	7
Reuben T. Whitaker; *S-44, Flasher*	18.5	5
Walter T. Griffith; *Bowfin, Bullhead*	17	5
Dudley W. Morton; *R-5, Wahoo*	17	6
John E. Lee; *S-12, Grayling, Croaker*	16	10
William B. Sieglaff; *Tautog, Tench*	15	7
Edward E. Shelby; *Sunfish*	14	5
Norvell G. Ward; *Guardfish*	14	5
Gordon W. Underwood; *Spadefish*	14	3
John S. Coye, Jr.; *Silversides*	14	6
Glynn R. Donaho; *Flying Fish, Picuda*	14	7
George E. Porter, Jr.; *Bluefish, Sennet*	14	6
Royce L. Gross; *Seawolf, Boarfish*	13.5	7
Henry G. Munson; *S-38, Crevalle, Rasher*	13	9
Robert E. Dornin; *Trigger*	13	3
Charles O. Triebel; *S-15, Snook*	13	8

The 20 Leading U-Boat Commanders

Commander/U-boat	Ships Sunk	Patrols
Otto Kretschmer; *U-23, U-19*	45	16
Wolfgang Luth; *U-9, U-138, U-43, U-181*	44	14
Jochim Schepko; *U-3, U-19, U-100*	39	14
Erich Topp; *U-57, U-552*	35	13
Victor Schutze; *U-25, U-103*	34	7
Heinrich Liebe; *U-38*	30	9
Karl F. Merten; *U-68*	29	5
Gunther Prien; *U-47*	29	10
Jochim Mohr; *U-124*	29	6
Georg Lassen; *U-160*	28	4
Carl Emmermann; *U-172*	27	5
Herbert Schultze; *U-48*	26	8
Werner Henke; *U-515*	26	6
Heinrich Bleichrodt; *U-48, U-109*	25	8
Robert Gysae; *U-98, U-177*	25	8
Klaus Scholtz; *U-108*	24	8
Reinhard Hardegen; *U-147, U-123*	23	—
H. L. Willenbroch; *U-5, U-96, U-256*	22	10
Engelbert Endrass; *U-46, U-567*	22	9
Ernst Kals; *U-130* (138,500 tons*)	19	5

*Kals had the highest gross tonnage among other commanders who sank 19 ships.

The 50 Leading Fighter Pilots of All Nations

The U.S. and most other nations did recognize the term "ace" as it applied to pilots who scored a minimum of five victories (or kills). Yet the term "ace" was, and still is, broadly used. As difficult as scoring five victories was, the list of all the aces of all nations would fill several pages. Various air forces counted victories differently. The U.S., Great Britain, Canada, Australia, and the other Allies for the most part included only enemy aircraft shot down in flight as a bona fide victory. Some countries counted planes on the ground, cars, trains, and so on; hence some of the celestial numbers. Fighter pilots listed here are the aces who earned the title *five times over or more*, meaning they scored a minimum of 25 victories. However, 38 German fighter aces are credited with 100 victories or more each. In the interest of brevity, only the German superaces with 250 or more victories each have been listed.

Fighter Ace	Nationality	Number of Victories	Fighter Ace	Nationality	Number of Victories
Erich Hartmann	Germany	352	Arsenii Vorozheikin	USSR	46
Gerhard Barkhorn	Germany	301	Niki Skomorokhov	USSR	46
Gunther Rall	Germany	275	Vasilii Kubarev	USSR	46
Otto Kittel	Germany	267	J. Pattle	S. Africa	41
Walther Nowotny	Germany	255	Richard I. Bong	U.S.	40
Hiroyishi Nishizawa	Japan	87*	Thomas B. McGuire	U.S.	38
Shoichi Sugita	Japan	80*	J. E. Johnson	Gr. Britain	38
Hans H. Wind	Finland	75	Cretian Galic	Yugoslavia	36
Saburo Saki	Japan	64†	A. G. Malan	S. Africa	35
Ivan Kozhedub	USSR	62	David McCampbell	U.S.	34
Alek Pokryshkin	USSR	59	P. H. Closterman	France	33
Grigorii Rechkalov	USSR	58	B. Finucane	Ireland	32
Hiromichi Shinohara	Japan	58	G. F. Beurling	Canada	31.5
Nikolai Gulaev	USSR	57	Frances S. Gabreski	U.S.	31
Waturo Nakamichi	Japan	55	J. R. D. Graham	Gr. Britain	29
Takeo Okumura	Japan	54	R. R. S. Tuck	Gr. Britain	29
Naoshi Kanno	Japan	52	C. R. Caldwell	Australia	28.5
Kirill Yevstigneev	USSR	52	Gregory Boyington	U.S.	28
Satoshi Anabuki	Japan	51	J. Frantisek	Czechoslovakia	28
Yasuhiko Kuroe	Japan	51	Robert S. Johnson	U.S.	28
Dimitrii Glinka	USSR	50	J. H. Lacey	Gr. Britain	28
Alexandr Klubov	USSR	50	C. F. Gray	New Zealand	27.5
Ivan Pilipenko	USSR	48	Charles H. MacDonald	U.S.	27
			George E. Preddy	U.S.	26
			E. S. Lock	Gr. Britain	26
			Joseph E. Foss	U.S.	26
			Robert M. Hanson	U.S.	25

*Some works credit Nishizawa with 103 kills and Sugita with 120.
†Sakai is credited with 80 kills in other works. However, this author is satisfied that the figures given here are correct. The discrepancies are pointed out because they do exist.

The 10 Fastest Fighter Planes in World War II

Between 1939–45, 64 different fighter planes were employed by Allied and Axis nations. Ranked by speed, here are the 10 fastest.

Aircraft	Country	Maximum Speed (mph)	Range (mi)
Messerschmitt-263	Germany	596 (rocket)	NA
Messerschmitt-262	Germany	560 (jet)	650
Heinkel He-162A	Germany	553	606
P-51-H	U.S.	487	850
Lavochkin La-11	USSR	460	466
Spitfire XIV	Britain	448	460
Yakovlev Yak-3	USSR	447	506
P-51-D Mustang	U.S.	440	2,300
Tempest VI	Britain	438	740
Focke-Wulf FW-190-D	Germany	435	560

If the list continued, other fighters would rank:
(12) P-47-D Thunderbolt, U.S. 428 mph
(14) F.4U Corsair, U.S. 417 mph
(16) P-38 Lightening, U.S. 414 mph
(19) Messerschmitt 109G, Germany, 400 mph

U.S. Navy Fleet Aircraft Carriers of World War II

The 1944–45 edition of *Jane's Fighting Ships* stated that the strength of the postwar 1946 U.S. Navy would be 18 battleships, 27 fleet aircraft carriers, and 79 escort aircraft carriers. The prewar rivalry between "the Gun Club" dreadnought admirals and the advocates of naval air power was over. The pendulum had swung dramatically in Hawaii on a December Sunday morning in 1941. The U.S. had eight aircraft carriers when it entered the war. By the time of the Japanese surrender in 1945 the Navy had added 113 more of all

types, including Fleet (CV), Light Fleet (CVL), and Escort (CVE). Listed here are only the CV carriers of World War II.

A trio of Large Fleet Aircraft Carriers (CVB) of 45,000 tons and 986 feet in overall length were laid down in 1943 and 1944 but were also not completed before the end of the war. They included USS *Midway* (CVB-41), USS *Franklin D. Roosevelt* (CVB-42), and USS *Coral Sea* (CVB-43). Orders for three others were cancelled in 1945.

Hull No.	Carrier	Completed	Tonnage	Length	Hull No.	Carrier	Completed	Tonnage	Length
CV-1	USS *Langley*	1922	12,903	519	CV-20	USS *Bennington*	1944	33,800	899
CV-2	USS *Lexington*	1927	49,500	909.5	CV-21	USS *Boxer*	1945	33,800	899
CV-3	USS *Saratoga*	1927	49,500	909.5	CV-31	USS *Bon Homme Richard*	1944	33,800	899
CV-4	USS *Ranger*	1934	14,500	769	CV-36	USS *Antietam*	1945	33,800	899
CV-5	USS *Yorktown*	1937	29,100	809.5	CV-38	USS *Shangri-La*	1944	33,800	899
CV-6	USS *Enterprise*	1938	29,100	809.5	CV-39	USS *Lake Champlain*	1944	33,800	899
CV-7	USS *Wasp*	1940	18,500	741	CV-32	USS *Leyte**			
CV-8	USS *Hornet*	1941	29,100	809.5	CV-33	USS *Kearsarge**			
CV-9	USS *Essex*	1942	33,800	899	CV-34	USS *Oriskany**			
CV-10	USS *Yorktown* (2nd)	1943	33,800	899	CV-37	USS *Princeton** (2)			
CV-11	USS *Intrepid*	1943	33,800	899	CV-40	USS *Tarawa**			
CV-12	USS *Hornet* (2nd)	1943	33,800	899	CV-45	USS *Valley Forge**			
CV-13	USS *Franklin*	1944	33,800	899	CV-47	USS *Philippine Sea**			
CV-14	USS *Ticonderoga*	1944	33,800	899					
CV-15	USS *Randolph*	1944	33,800	899					
CV-16	USS *Lexington* (2nd)	1943	33,800	899					
CV-17	USS *Bunker Hill*	1943	33,800	899					
CV-18	USS *Wasp* (2nd)	1943	33,800	899					
CV-19	USS *Hancock*	1944	33,800	899					

*These last seven *Essex*-class carriers were commissioned after hostilities ended. The *Essex* class originally called for 36 *Essex*-size carriers. Twelve other carriers were cancelled in March and August 1945.

U.S. Navy and Coast Guard Ships at Pearl Harbor, December 7, 1941

Although most references agree that there were 96 warships in Pearl Harbor during the Japanese attack and that 18 of them were sunk, it is rarely mentioned that the U.S. Navy and Coast Guard had 49 other ships there at the time. The complete list of 145 ships present, reading across alphabetically, includes:

Advocet (AVP-4)	Allen (DD-66)	Alywin (DD-335)	PT-24	PT-25	PT-26
Antares (AKE-3)	Argone (AG-31)	Arizona (BB-39)	PT-27	PT-28	PT-29
Ash (YN-2)	Bagley (DD-386)	Blue (DD-387)	PT-30	PT-42	Pyro (AE-1)
Bobolink (AM-20)	Breese (DM-18)	Cachalot (SS-170)	Rail (AM-26)	Raleigh (CL-7)	Ralph Talbot (DD-390)
California (BB-44)	Case (DD-370)	Cassin (DD-372)	Ramapo (AO-12)	Ramsay (DM-16)	Reedbird (AMc-30)
Castor (AKS-1)	CG-8 (USCG)	Chengho (IX-52)	Reid (DD-369)	Reliance (USCG)	Rigel (AR-11)
Chew (DD-106)	Cinchona (YN-7)	Cockatoo AMc-9)	Sacramento (PG-19)	St. Louis (CL-49)	San Francisco (CA-38)
Cockenoe (YN-47)	Condor (AMc-14)	Conyngham (DD-371)	Schley (DD-103)	Selfridge (DD-357)	Shaw (DD-373)
Crossbill (AMc-9)	Cummings (DD-365)	Curtiss (AV-4)	Sicard (DM-21)	Solace (AH-5)	Sotoyomo (YT-9)
Dale (DD-353)	Detroit (CL-8)	Dewey (DD-349)	Sumner (AG-32)	Sunnadin (AT-28)	Swan (AVP-7)
Dobbin (AD-3)	Dolphin (SS-169)	Downes (DD-375)	Taney (PG-37)†	Tangier (AV-8)	Tautog (SS-199)
Farragut (DD-348)	Gamble (DM-15)	Grebe (AM-43)	Tennessee (BB-43)	Tern (AM-31)	Thornton (AVD-11)
Helena (CL-50)	Helm (CL-50)	Henley (DD-391)	Tiger (PC-152)	Tracy (DM-19)	Trever (DMS-16)
Hoga (YT-146)	Honolulu (Cl-48)	Hulbert (AVD-6)	Tucker (DD-374)	Turkey (AM-13)	Utah (AG-16)
Hull (DD-350)	Jarvis (DD-393)	Keosangua (AT-38)	Vega (AK-17)	Vestal (Ar-4)	Vireo (AM-52)
MacDonough (DD-351)	Manuwai (YFB-17)	Marin (YN-53)	Wapello (YN-56)	Ward (DD-139)	Wasmuth (DMS-15)
Maryland (BB-46)	Medusa (AR-1)	Monaghan (DD-354)	West Virginia (BB-48)	Whitney (AD-4)	Widgeon (ASR-1)
Montgomery (DM-17)	Mugford (DD-389)	Narwhal (SS-167)	Worden (DD-352)	YG-15	YG-17
Navajo (AT-64)	Neosho (AO-23)	Nevada (BB-36)	YG-21	YMT-5	YNa-17
New Orleans (CA-32)	Nokomis (YT-142)	Oglala (CM-4)	YO-21	YO-30	YO-43
Oklahoma (BB-37)	Ontario (AT-13)	Osceola (YT-129)	YO-44	YP-108	YP-109
Patterson (DD-392)	Pelias (AS-14)	Pennsylvania (BB-38)	YT-3	YT-119	YT-130
Perry (DMS-17)	Phelps (DD-360)	Phoenix (CL-46)*	YT-152	YT-153	YW-16
Preble (DM-20)	Pruitt (DM-22)	PT-20	Zane (DMS-14)		
PT-21	PT-22	PT-23			

*The USS Phoenix, as noted elsewhere in this book, was sold to Argentina in 1951 and renamed the General Belgrano. She became the first ship sunk by a submarine since the end of World War II when she was hit by a British torpedo on May 2, 1982, during the Falkland Islands war.

†The USS Taney, a 327-foot-long endurance cutter, remained on active U.S. service into the 1980s, longer than any other ship present at Pearl Harbor on December 7, 1941.

KIDO BUTAI—THE IMPERIAL JAPANESE NAVY PEARL HARBOR STRIKE FORCE

The Japanese fleet that left its home waters in November 1941 and steamed toward its infamous rendezvous with America consisted of 22 surface warships, eight oiler and supply ships, and 30 submarines, 60 ships total. All but three of them would be sunk during the course of the war. The trio of survivors included the destroyer *Ushio* and submarine *I–21*, which both surrendered, and the oiler *Kyokuto Maru*.

	Warships	Subsequent Fate	Date of Action		Warships	Subsequent Fate	Date of Action
CV	*Akagi*	Sunk, Midway	5 June 1942	SS	I-8	Sunk, Okinawa	31 Mar. 1945
CV	*Kaga*	Sunk, Midway	4 June 1942	SS	I-9	Sunk, Aleutians	11 June 1943
CVL	*Hiryu*	Sunk, Midway	5 June 1942	SS	I-10	Sunk, Saipan	4 July 1944
CVL	*Soryu*	Sunk, Midway	4 June 1942	SS	I-15	Sunk, Guadalcanal	2 Nov. 1942
CV	*Shokaku*	Sunk, Philippine Sea	19 June 1944	SS	I-16	Sunk, Solomon Islands	19 May 1944
CV	*Zuikaku*	Sunk, Leyte Gulf	25 Oct. 1944	SS	I-17	Sunk, Nouméa	19 Aug. 1943
BB	*Hiei*	Sunk, Guadalcanal	13 Nov. 1942	SS	I-18	Sunk, Guadalcanal	11 Feb. 1943
BB	*Kirishima*	Sunk, Guadalcanal	15 Nov. 1942	SS	I-19	Sunk, unknown causes	Oct. 1943
CA	*Chikuma*	Sunk, Leyte Gulf	25 Oct. 1944	SS	I-20	Sunk, New Hebrides	16 Sept. 1943
CA	*Tone*	Sunk, Kure	24 July 1945	SS	I-21	Surrendered	
CL	*Abukuma*	Sunk, Leyte Gulf	26 Oct. 1944	SS	I-22	Sunk, unknown causes	Oct. 1942
DD	*Akigumo*	Sunk, Philippines	11 Apr. 1944	SS	I-23	Sunk, Guadalcanal	29 Aug. 1942
DD	*Arare*	Sunk, Aleutians	5 July 1942	SS	I-24	Sunk, Aleutians	11 June 1943
DD	*Asakaze*	Sunk, Philippines	23 Aug. 1944	SS	I-25	Sunk, New Hebrides	3 Sept. 1943
DD	*Hamakaze*	Sunk, Okinawa	7 Apr. 1945	SS	I-26	Sunk, Philippines	Oct. 1944
DD	*Kagero*	Sunk, Solomon Islands	8 May 1943	SS	I-68	Sunk, Bismarck Sea	27 July 1943
DD	*Kasumi*	Sunk, Okinawa	7 Apr. 1945	SS	I-69	Sunk, Truk	4 Apr. 1944
DD	*Shiranumi*	Sunk, Leyte Gulf	27 Oct. 1944	SS	I-70	Sunk, Pearl Harbor	10 Dec. 1941
DD	*Tanikaze*	Sunk, Philippines	9 June 1944	SS	I-71	Sunk, Solomon Islands	1 Feb. 1944
DD	*Urakaze*	Sunk, Formosa	21 Nov. 1944	SS	I-72	Sunk, Guadalcanal	11 Nov. 1942
DD	*Sazanami*	Sunk, Yap	14 Jan. 1944	SS	I-73	Sunk, Midway	27 Jan. 1942
DD	*Ushio*	Surrendered		SS	I-74	Sunk, unknown causes	Apr. 1944
SS	I-1	Sunk, Guadalcanal	29 Jan. 1943	SS	I-75	Sunk, Marshall Islands	1 Feb. 1944
SS	I-2	Sunk, Bismarck Sea	7 July 1944				
SS	I-3	Sunk, Guadalcanal	10 Dec. 1942				

Oilers and Supply Ships

SS	I-4	Sunk, Guadalcanal	20 Dec. 1942
SS	I-5	Sunk, Guam	19 July 1944

Seven of the eight oiler and supply ships were lost in various actions. As noted, only *Kyokuto Maru* survived. The eight were:

SS	I-6	Sunk, unknown causes	June 1944
SS	I-7	Sunk, Aleutians	5 July 1943[1]

Kyokuto Maru	Kyokuyo Maru	Kenyo Maru	Kokuyo
Shinkoku Maru	Toho Maru	Toei Maru	Nippon Maru

Fate of the Officers of the Pearl Harbor Strike Force

Several of the Japanese officers involved in planning or executing the attack were also absent from the surrender ceremonies in Tokyo Bay 46 months later:

- Admiral Isoroku Yamamoto, the senior officer who insisted that any war with the U.S. begin with the destruction of the U.S. fleet at Pearl Harbor, was in Tokyo when hostilities began. He was killed when the plane he was in was shot down over Bougainville on April 18, 1943.
- The strike force commander and senior Imperial Japanese Navy officer present during the attack was Vice Admiral Chuichi Nagumo. He was killed in action at Saipan.
- Rear Admiral Tamon Yamaguchi, commander in chief, 2nd Carrier Division, and two aircraft carrier captains who had been part of the Pearl Harbor attack force bound themselves to parts of their ships and went down with them during the Battle of Midway rather than abandon the carriers. Yamaguchi and Captain Tomeo Kaku died with the *Hiru*, and Captain Taijiro Aoki went down with the *Akagi*.

- Rear Admiral Matome Ugake, chief of staff to Yamamoto and the man who wrote the historic "Climb Mount Niitaka" message signaling the irrevocable order to attack Pearl Harbor, died piloting a kamikaze on the *last day* of the war.
- Lieutenant Commander Shigeru Itaya, leader of the fighters in the first wave, was accidentally killed by friendly fire over the Kuriles.
- Lieutenant Commander Shigemaru Murata, the torpedo bomber leader in the first wave, was killed in action at Santa Cruz on October 26, 1942.
- Lieutenant Commander Kakuiche Takahashi, leader of the dive bombers in the first wave, was killed in action on May 2, 1942, during the Battle of the Coral Sea.
- Lieutenant Commander Shigekazu Shimazaki, commander of the second-wave attack force, was killed in action over the Philippines on January 9, 1945.
- Lieutenant Commander Takashige Egusa, leader of the dive bombers in the second wave, was killed over Saipan.

How to Apply for the Pearl Harbor Medal

Military personnel and civilians who participated in the defense of Hawaii during the December 7, 1941, Japanese attack are eligible for a bronze medal that will be presented to the survivors or their next of kin on or about the 50th anniversary of the attack in 1991.

On November 5, 1990, Public Law 101-511 provided for the striking of approximately 50,000 bronze medals known as the Pearl Harbor Defender's Medal. The law authorized the Speaker of the House of Representatives and the president pro tempore of the Senate to present a 1.5-inch-diameter medal to persons determined to be eligible. The secretary of defense is required by law to provide them with a list of eligible names by November 5, 1991. Medals may be accepted by the next of kin of people killed in action during the

attack or who have since died.

To establish eligibility, a person or the next of kin must present to the Secretary of Defense an application with supporting documentation that the individual for whom the medal is being sought was involved as a member of the military or as a civilian employee of the War Department or the Department of the Navy in responding to the attack. If more than one relative or next of kin of a deceased individual files an application for the medal, the secretary will determine which one receives the medal.

To receive an application or determine eligibility contact the Department of Defense toll-free at (800) 545-4052.

ALLIED AND AXIS TANKS

The major warring nations used no less than 31 different tank models in combat between 1939–45. The smallest was the Italian L3, which, at 3.4 tons and 10 feet, five inches long accommodated a two-man crew. The largest by far was the German Tiger II. At 33 feet, nine inches long and tipping the scales at 74.8 tons, it required a five-man crew. The second-largest tank, the German Elephant, also at 74.8 tons but only 22.3 feet long, had a six-man crew. The U.S. M3 was the only other tank with a six-man crew. There were, however, several smaller tanks with five-man crews.

Country/Tank	Weight (tons)	Length (feet)	Number Built
German; PzKpfw Tiger II	74.8	33.9	485
German; PzKpfw Elephant	74.8	22.3	90
German; PzKpfw Tiger I	62.7	27.9	1,350
Soviet; KVIA Kliment	52	22	10,000
German; PzKpfw Panther	50	33.1	384
German; PzKpfw V	49.3	29	3,740
Soviet; JSH Joseph Stalin	45.3	32.2	Unknown
British; Mark IV Churchill	43.1	24.5	5,640
U.S.; M26 Pershing	41.1	28.10	2,428
U.S.; M4A3 Sherman	37.1	19.3	49,000
Soviet; T34/85	34.5	20.2	Unknown
Soviet; SU85	32.4	26.8	Unknown
U.S.; M3 (Lee & Grant models)	31	18.6	4,924
British; Mark VIII Cromwell	30.8	20.10	1,000+
Soviet; T34/76	29.7	21.7	40,000
British; Mark IIA Matilda	29.7	18.5	2,987
German; PzKpfw III	24.5	17.9	5,650
British; Mark VI Crusader	22.1	19.7	5,300
German; PzKpfw IV	19.7	19.4	6,000
British; Mark III Valentine	17.9	17.9	8,275
German; PzKpfw Chaser	17.6	20.7	1,577
Japanese; 97 Chi-Ha	15.6	18.1	1,000+
Italian; model Mi3/40	15.4	16.2	2,000
U.S.; M3a1 Stuart	14.3	14.10	4,621
Japanese; 89B Chi-Ro	12.8	18.1	1,000+
Italian; model 11/39	10.8	15.6	100
Soviet; T26	10.1	15.3	4,500
German; PzKpfw II	9.35	15.9	650
Japanese; 95 Ha-Go	7.5	14.4	2,464
British; Mark VIa	5.7	13.2	1,000+
Italian; L3	3.4	10.5	2,500

World War II Ship Memorials and Their Locations

Battleships		
USS *Alabama*	(BB-60)	Mobile, Ala.
USS *Arizona*	(BB-39)	Pearl Harbor, Oahu, Hawaii
USS *Massachusetts*	(BB-59)	Fall River, Mass.
USS *Missouri*	(BB-63)	Bremerton, Wash.
USS *North Carolina*	(BB-55)	Wilmington, N.C.
USS *Texas*	(BB-35)	La Porte, Tex.
USS *Utah*	(BB-31)	Pearl Harbor, Oahu, Hawaii

Submarines		
USS *Batfish*	(SS-310)	Muskogee, Okla.
USS *Becuna*	(SS-319)	Philadelphia, Pa.
USS *Bowfin*	(SS-287)	Honolulu, Hawaii
USS *Cavalla*	(SS-244)	Galveston, Tex.
USS *Cobia*	(SS-245)	Manitowoc, Wis.
USS *Codd*	(SS-224)	Cleveland, Ohio
USS *Croaker*	(SS-246)	Groton, Conn.
USS *Ling*	(SS-297)	Hackensack, N.J.
USS *Pampanito*	(SS-383)	San Francisco, Calif.
USS *Requin*	(SS-481)	Tampa, Fla.
USS *Silversides*	(SS-236)	Chicago, Ill.
USS *Torsk*	(SS-423)	Baltimore, Md.
U-505 (captured German sub)		Chicago, Ill.

Other ships		
USS *Intrepid*	(CV-11)	New York, N.Y.
USS *Yorktown*	(CV-10)	Charleston, S.C.
USS *Kidd*	(DD-661)	Baton Rouge, La.
USS *Stewart*	(DE-238)	Galveston, Tex.
USS *The Sullivans*	(DDG-537)	Buffalo, N.Y.
USS *Inaugural*	(AM-242)	St. Louis, Mo.
USS *Hazard*	(AM-240)	Omaha, Nebr.
USS *Little Rock*	(CLG-4)	Buffalo, N.Y.
PT-619		Memphis, Tenn.

INDEX